TREKKING IN THE APENNINES

About the Author

Gillian Price was born in England but moved to Australia when young. After taking a degree in anthropology and working in adult education, she set off to travel through Asia and trek the Himalayas. The culmination of her journey was Venice where, her enthusiasm for mountains fired, the next logical step was towards the Dolomites, only hours away. Starting there, Gillian is steadily exploring the mountain ranges of Italy and bringing them to life for visitors in a series of outstanding guides for Cicerone. When not out walking and photographing with her Venetian cartographer husband, Gillian works as a writer and translator. An adamant promoter of the use of public transport to minimise impact in alpine areas, she is an active member of the Italian Alpine Club and the Outdoor Writers' Guild.

Other Cicerone guides by Gillian Price
Walking in the Dolomites
Walking in the Central Italian Alps
Walking in Italy's Gran Paradiso
Walking in Tuscany
Walking in Sicily
Shorter Walks in the Dolomites
Treks in the Dolomites: Alte Vie 1 & 2 (co-author)
Walking on Corsica

TREKKING IN THE APENNINES

GEA – Grande Escursione Appenninica

by
Gillian Price

© Gillian Price 2005
ISBN 1 85284 416 7
A catalogue record for this book is available from the British Library

Maps by Nicola Regine (with gratitude)

Acknowledgements

Heaps of thanks to Anna, Colleen, Daniele and Nick for their immensely enjoyable company on the trail, the woodcutters and hunters who pointed us in the right direction, CAI branches for practical information and the *rifugi* cooks for their delectable bilberry tarts.

Thanks to Jonathan the publisher, who said 'yes' once again, and the team at Cicerone who put the book together. Lastly I am indebted to Giorgio Baruffini of Parma for his help with those place name explanations that so intrigue me.

Advice to Readers

Readers are advised that while every effort is taken by the author to ensure the accuracy of this guidebook, changes can occur which may affect the contents. It is also advisable to check locally on transport, accommodation, shops, etc.

The author would welcome information on any updates and changes. Please send to the author care of Cicerone Press, 2 Police Square, Milnthorpe, Cumbria LA7 7PY

Front cover: Descending to Passo di Badignana (Stage 20)

CONTENTS

Sketch Map Legend

━━━━━	motorway	⬆	hotel, rifugio, posto tappa
═══════	sealed road	⬈	unmanned refuge or bivacco
┼┼┼┼┼┼┼┼	railway	✝	church or shrine
─ ─ ─ ─ ─	walk route	⬭	lake
....	walk variant	⬆	chairlift

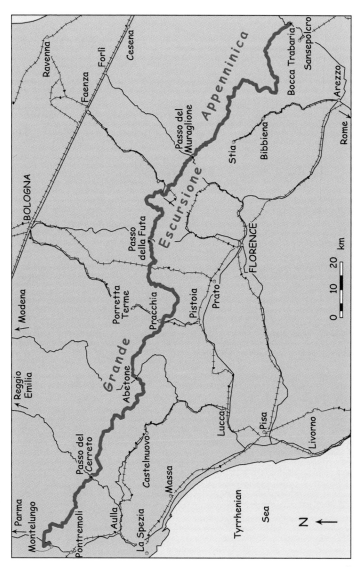

7

En route to Monte La Nuda (Stage 20)

INTRODUCTION

Your peaks are beautiful, ye Apennines!
In the soft light of these serenest skies;
From the broad highland region, black with pines,
Fair as the hills of Paradise they rise.

(*To the Apennines*, William Cullen Bryant, 1835)

THE APENNINES

The mountainous Apennines are without a doubt Italy's best-kept secret. For walkers this glorious range provides thousands of kilometres of marked walking trails over stunning panoramic ridges and explores stupendous forested valleys and quiet communities, little affected by tourism. There are nature reserves with plentiful wildlife and marvellous wild flowers, historic sanctuaries, hospitable mountain inns, incredible roads and passes that testify to feats of engineering, and stark memorials to the terrible events of World War II.

The Apennines form the rugged spine of the slender Italian peninsula, giving it body and support as it ventures out into the Mediterranean. Peaking at 2912m, the range runs northwest–southeast along the entire length of the country and clocks up some 1400km (870 miles) from its link with the Alps close to the French border, all the way south to the Strait of Messina, even extending over to Sicily. As a formidable barrier that splits Italy in two lengthways, the Apennines have witnessed centuries of wars and skirmishes, alternating with the passage of traders, pilgrims and daring bandits.

The rock is, by and large, sedimentary in nature – sandstone, shale and some limestone – deposited in an ancient sea during the Mesozoic era (245–66 million years ago). The mountains came into existence in the immediate aftermath of their neighbours, the Alps, when remnants of the African plate were forced and squeezed upwards little by little, starting 66 million years ago and climaxing around 2 million years ago.

In the southern regions ongoing volcanic and seismic activity continue to shape the mountains while – though glaciers are now completely absent from the Apennines – ancient ice masses have left much evidence of their existence. One tell-tale clue are the smoothed rock surfaces which, when examined close-to, reveal a host of scratches, caused by stones dragged along by the moving ice. However the easiest to identify are the multitudinous cirques, like giant armchairs found below high ridges, once filled by ice from a lateral glacier tongue and nowadays home more often than not to a lake or tarn. These

Wisps of cloud on Cima dell'Omo (Stage 17)

appear mostly in the northern Apennines and face north-northeast, the colder sheltered face. Over time many have steadily accumulated layers of rotting vegetation which are compressed into stratified peat bogs. These in turn dry out, making way for meadows, and eventually woodland.

The present overall aspect of the Apennines – steep, rough western flanks overlooking the Tyrrhenian Sea, in contrast to the gentler slopes on the eastern Adriatic side – is due mainly to recent erosion by water. Over time the inhospitable land, scarcity of water and lack of minerals have severely limited human settlement on any substantial scale. But despite this evidence has been unearthed of man's presence since prehistoric times, some 7000 years ago. At that time the northern Apennines were the stronghold of the ancient Liguri or Ligurian people (as the colonising Romans found out to their detriment over the 150 years it took to

get the fierce resisters to accept domination). Their heritage is evident today mainly via fascinating place names and anthropomorphic stone sculptures, similar to those in Corsica. We are probably indebted to these primitive people for the very name Apennines: the root 'penn' signified an isolated peak, a denomination found throughout Italy. In another version (less credited in this day and age) Pennine was a divinity believed to reside on the inhospitable summits, while a further interpretation attributes the name to Re Api, last of the Italic gods.

Over time well-trodden paths conveyed waves of passers-by, such as devotees on the Via Francigena which led from Canterbury to Rome and beyond. The great medieval poet Dante Alighieri spent part of his exile from his native Florence in the Apennines. It was a source of inspiration for the *Divine Comedy,* and the same holds true for Petrarch and

Boccaccio. Brilliant German writer and traveller Johann Wolfgang von Goethe, revelling in sun-blessed Italy, was heading south towards Rome in October 1786, and wrote:

> I find the Apennines a remarkable part of the world. Upon the great plain of the Po basin there follows a mountain range that rises from the depths, between two seas, to end the continent on the south… it is a curious web of mountain ridges facing each other… if the valleys were filled in more and the flat surfaces smoother and better watered, the region could be compared to Bohemia, except that these mountains have an entirely different character. Still, one must not imagine a high wasteland, but a countryside most cultivated, even though mountainous.

From their base near the Tyrrhenian coast, both Mary and Percy Bysshe Shelley were inspired by the Apennines, which made appearances in their respective works *Valperga* and *The Witch of Atlas*.

The 'romantic' wild woods and mountainous ridges were long the realm of smugglers, woodcutters and charcoal burners. The latter were renowned as a wild mob who moved from camp to camp erecting huge compact mounds of cut branches that underwent slow round-the-clock combustion. Their circular cleared work platforms are still visible. It's also common to encounter monuments to the passage of indefatigable Giuseppe Garibaldi, responsible for uniting the north of Italy with Sicily and the southern regions in 1861 under the Kingdom of the House of Savoy. He crossed the Apennines on one of his campaigns, his ranks swelled by several of the Robin Hood-style bandits in revolt in the Romagna region against harsh taxes and the Austrian occupation.

The central-north section of the Apennines were subjected to widespread devastation in the latter years of World War II. Once fascist Italy had recapitulated and signed a peace agreement with the Allies in 1943, the Germans turned into occupying forces and dug themselves in to prepare for the inevitable Allied advance. They constructed massive defences – the so-called Gothic Line – that stretched coast-to-coast all the way across the peninsula, drastically clearing ridges to enable control of strategic passes and key communication routes such as railways. Now a sea of green has all but obliterated signs of battle, so present-day visitors perceive little of this. However, there are poignant reminders in the shape of war cemeteries and ubiquitous memorials to the partisans, former soldiers who sprang into action after the armistice, aided in numerous cases by Allied officers parachuted in behind the lines.

A final note is in order pertaining to emigration. Starting at the end of the 19th century entire villages the length and breadth of

11

the Apennines were abandoned as people left in search of work in France, Belgium, Germany and the UK, often to labour in the mines. In many cases the links with 'home' were never severed, and apparently deserted hamlets in isolated spots swell and come to life during the summer months as relatives return to open up the old family home and enjoy the cool mountain air. A multitude of languages can be heard, and foreign number plates spotted.

THE TREK

The trek described in this guide is a walk along the central mountainous spine of Italy, a journey through a vast wooded swathe of the country, miles from the well-beaten tourist trail. The villages and passes encountered see few domestic let alone foreign visitors.

The Trek spends 23 wonderful days (a grand total of 123 hours 35 minutes) snaking its way northwest along the ridge of the central-north Apennines with numerous diversions to valley-based villages. It follows (for the main part) the established long-distance walking route known as the GEA (pronounced 'jayah' in Italian), which stands for Grande Escursione Appenninica. Conceived in the 1980s by Florentine walking enthusiasts Alfonso Bietolini and Gianfranco Bracci, it has since been incorporated into the mammoth Sentiero Italia (SI) project and the European trail E1.

However, during preparations for this guide, departures from the original route became necessary at numerous points along the way due to impassable overgrown tracks, absence of waymarking and the creeping advance of tarmac, in addition to logical improvements.

Starting in eastern Tuscany on the border with Umbria and the Marche, it makes a number of forays into Emilia-Romagna – with marked changes in accents and cuisine – and moves across to run parallel to the Tyrrhenian Sea heading north to the edge of Liguria. A little under 400km in length (375.6km – about a third of the total length of the Apennine chain), it entails altitudes ranging between 400 and 2000m above sea level. With accommodation in comfortable guest houses and refuges, it is suitable for a broad range of walkers.

The route is straightforward, on well-marked paths and forestry tracks. The odd brief tract negotiates exposed crest, usually avoidable. The terrain ranges from thick carpets of flowered meadows through to rock slopes and woods, where layers of leaf litter provide a soft base for tired feet and the plays of sunlight serve as distractions from fatigue.

The initial southernmost sections of the Trek traverse the multi-star 364 sq km Parco Nazionale delle Foreste Casentinesi, which boasts magnificent spreads of ancient chestnut, fir and beech wood lovingly nurtured by monks over the centuries. Moreover it

Red/white paint markings are constant companions

New generation columns make for clear waymarking

coincides with the pathways taken by St Francis of Assisi as he tramped the hills setting up isolated retreats and spreading his message of simplicity. The second, higher part of the Trek makes its rocky way 'on a tightrope' high above Tuscany and Emilia-Romagna, where noteworthy localities stand out. On the eastern flanks, where the Apennines slope down to the intensively cultivated Po plain, is the city of Parma, renowned for cured ham and world-famous Parmesan cheese; then there's Modena, synonymous with balsamic vinegar. On the opposite side of the Apennines, to the west, is Carrara and the Apuan Alps, heavily quarried for the high-grade marble transformed into Italy's masterpieces by artists the likes of Michelangelo. On the other hand the actual ridges traversed come under the auspices of the brand new

240 sq km Parco Nazionale dell'Appennino Tosco-Emiliano, which has brought together two high-profile regional parks, the Parco del Gigante and Parco dei Cento Laghi, not to mention four special state reserves.

WHEN TO GO

Although the climate in the Apennines is classified as continental, it is subject to the warming influence of the Mediterranean. Summers are generally hot and winters freezing cold, though temperatures are mitigated by altitude: average figures given are 2°C in January and 22°C in July. Abundant snowfalls can be expected from December through to March/April. Thereafter it turns into rain, heavier on the Tyrrhenian side than the Adriatic on account of the

View towards Monte Prado and Monte Cusna (Stage 18)

moisture-laden winds which blow straight in from the nearby sea.

The Trek was originally designed as a summer itinerary: July–August is the perfect time to go with guaranteed stable conditions and all accommodation and transport operating. Having said that, it is important to add that – with an eye on hotel/refuge availability – any time from April through to October is both possible and highly recommended. Early springtime can be divine with fresh, crisp air, well ahead of summer's mugginess. It's also a great time to go wildlife watching as the lack of foliage facilitates viewing. Disadvantages at this time of year may include snow cover above the 1500m mark if winter falls have come late, and even the odd flurry, though waterproof gaiters and extra care in orientation can help cope with that.

May usually brings perfect walking weather, neither too hot nor too cold, though some rain is to be expected. Late September–October is simply glorious, with mile after mile of beech wood at its russet best. On the downside, low-lying cloud and mist are more likely in this season. Encounters with amateur hunters can also be expected in late autumn. Solitary optimists after tiny birds (on an illegal basis more often than not) will mostly be camouflaged and dug into hides on ridges and clearings – a polite greeting such as *Buon giorno* (Good day) is in order to alert them to your presence. (The chaotic large-scale boar hunts are not held until the midwinter months.)

Walking any later than November will increase the chance of inclement weather and hotel closure. The majority of small towns and villages have one hotel operating year-round, but these sometimes restrict themselves to weekends and public holidays in the off-season. Moreover, with the end of Daylight Savings at the end of October the days will be too short for the longer stages.

In terms of transport and accommodation, with the odd exception, it is safe to say that Stages 1–13 are suitable from spring through to autumn, whereas the latter part (Stages 14–23) is limited to midsummer as the higher altitude refuges don't start opening until June.

In terms of Italian public holidays, in addition to the Christmas–New Year period and Easter, people (bus drivers included) have time off on 6 January, 25 April, 1 May, 2 June, 15 August, 1 November and 8 December.

With the exception of midsummer at hot spots (such as the lakes in the later stages) few other walkers are to be expected apart from local clubs on weekends or the odd school group in the Casentino Park. Otherwise in autumn you might come across mushroom collectors or hunters, who know the terrain like the back of their hand, as well as trail-bike and horse riders.

ACCESS

By **plane** the handiest international airports are Ancona, Bologna, Forlì, Pescara, Pisa and Rome, each with ongoing public transport (trains and buses) to the walk start.

The road pass Bocca Trabaria, where the Trek begins, can be reached by **public transport** from either side of the mountainous Apennine ridge as follows: long-distance Bucci coaches run between Sansepolcro and the Adriatic coastal town of Pesaro on a daily basis (except Sundays and holidays), while Baschetti do a Sansepolcro–Urbino run on Mondays and Fridays during the school term. Sansepolcro can be reached by train from Perugia, not to mention by frequent year-round bus from Arezzo, on the main Florence–Rome railway line.

By **car** one possibility is to leave Italy's main north–south *autostrada* A1 motorway in the Val di Chiana at the Arezzo exit. Then the *strada statale* SS73 will take you to Sansepolcro for the subsequent tortuous switchbacks of the SS73bis climbing over to Bocca Trabaria. Otherwise from the A14 following Italy's Adriatic coast, exit at Pesaro for the SS73bis via Urbino and

Signposts at Passo della Cisa (Stage 23)

head inland for the climb to Bocca Trabaria. While it would be possible to take a series of trains and buses in order to return to pick up your car at the pass afterwards, it may not be safe to leave it unattended at such an isolated sport for any long period. It would also appear more logical to leave it at a transport hub such as Sansepolcro. Hotels can help with long-term parking suggestions.

The Trek's conclusion is at the village of Montelungo, pick-up point for the CAT bus to the railway station at Pontremoli. Then you're in for a short journey west to the Tuscany-Liguria coast and La Spezia, alternately north-east to Parma and the Po plain.

PUBLIC TRANSPORT

As the Apennines have been criss-crossed since time immemorial by tracks and roads of all sorts linking the Adriatic coast to the Tyrrhenian, the Trek encounters a multitude of road passes and settlements served by buses and the odd train. This makes it especially versatile for fitting in with requisites of shorter holidays or unfavourable weather. The capillary network is reliable, reasonably priced and generally punctual. Details of public transport are given at relevant points during the walk description.

The information given here was checked at the time of writing. However modifications are inevitable, so where possible consult the relevant website for up-to-date information.

For timetable enquiries for the Italian State railway network telephone 892021 (voice-activated, Italian only); or go to **www.trenitalia.com**.

The relevant bus companies, and zones they cover, are:

Waves of wild wooded ridges en route to Rifugio Pacini (Stage 12)

- ACT tel: 0522 431667 Reggio Emilia district www.actre.it
- ATC tel: 051 290290 Bologna environs www.atc.bo.it
- ATCM tel: 199 111101 Modena region www.atcm.mo.it
- ATR tel: 0543 27821 Forlì hinterland www.atr-online.it
- Baschetti tel: 0575 749816 does an Arezzo–Sansepolcro–Bocca Trabaria–Urbino run, but only on Mondays and Fridays during the school term. www.baschetti.it/servizi.htm
- Bucci tel: 0721 32401 has a daily Arezzo–Sansepolcro–Bocca Trabaria–Urbino service, year-round except Sunday and holidays.
- CAP tel: 0574 6081 does the surrounds of Prato www.capautolinee.it
- CAT tel: 800 223010 (free phone) for the Pontremoli district.
- CLAP tel: 0583 587897) covers the Castiglione di Garfagnana–Passo delle Radici and San Pellegrino runs.
- COPIT tel: 800 277825 (free phone) is responsible for the Pistoia province www.copitspa.it
- FCU tel: 075 5729121 for the Perugia–Sansepolcro railway www.fcu.it
- LFI tel: 0575 39881 covers the buses in the Casentino National Park as well as a branch railway line from Arezzo via Bibbiena and terminating at Stia.

- SITA tel: 800 373760 (free phone), the main bus company for the whole of Tuscany, serves Sansepolcro and surrounding villages and towns www.sita-on-line.it
- TEP tel: 800 977966 (free phone) has services all over the Parma province. www.tep.pr.it In addition, its ground-breaking Pronto Bus tel: 800 977900 (free phone) can be contacted (preferably the day before) to arrange for pick-ups at mountain localities (for instance Passo della Cisa) not covered by the regular lines, costing the equivalent of a normal fare.

Useful travel and timetable terminology can be found below:

biglietto di andata (andata-ritorno)	single (return) ticket
cambio a coincidenza	change at connection
feriale	working days ie Mon to Sat
festivo	Sundays and public holidays
giornaliero	daily
sciopero	strike
scolastico	schooldays
soppresso	no service
da… a…	from… to…(dates)

Rifugio Mariotti at Lago Santo Modenese is a must (Stage 22)

Bus tickets should usually be purchased beforehand – usually at a café, newspaper kiosk or tobacconist in the vicinity of the bus stop, and stamped on board. Where this is not possible just get on and ask the driver, though you may be charged a modest surcharge.

HOW TO USE THIS GUIDE

To aid planning the route has been divided into stages, which correspond roughly to days. Each concludes somewhere with accommodation and meals. However, individual walkers have their own pace and there is no reason why stages should not be longer or shorter. The Route Summary at the end of the guide has been provided for this purpose. All intermediate points with facilities such as accommodation and public transport are listed to facilitate variations.

The **timing** given does NOT include stops for rest, lunch and taking photographs, so always add on

an extra hour or so when planning your day. A load of 4–5 hours is quite sufficient for starters. Moreover midsummer walkers should allow for the inevitably frequent pauses to gather – and consume – the prolific bilberries and raspberries.

When 'path' is used it means a narrow pedestrians-only route, whereas a 'lane' or 'track' is a wider unsurfaced track, and a 'road' is sealed and used by traffic, unless specified differently. Roads are often referred to with their Italian code, ie SS (*strada statale*, national road) or SP (*strada provinciale*, provincial road) followed by a number.

Difficulty is expressed as grades:
- **Grade 1:** straightforward walking with little ascent on a forestry track or broad clear path, and problem-free terrain; suitable for first-timers.

- **Grade 2:** moderate difficulty over mountainous terrain or considerable height gain.

• **Grade 3:** strenuous routes entailing exposed stretches, basic orientation skills preferable.

Metres expressed as 'm' (not to be confused with 'min', short for minutes) are used for altitude readings, and of course on all commercial maps in Italy. NB: 100m = 328ft.

Another essential piece of information given in the stage headings is height gain and loss, ie overall **ascent and descent**: this means the total amount of metres the Trek climbs and drops during that stage. This information is often a more useful key to the day's walk load than actual distance. On the other hand the kilometre/mile readings listed are only approximate due to the inaccuracy inherent in measuring mountainous routes on relatively simplified maps. In any case they do give a helpful idea of the distance involved.

Route descriptions include the use of right (R) and left (L), accompanied by compass bearings abbreviated as S, N, NW and so forth.

Local path numbering is referred to where relevant, according to the nationwide system of the Italian Alpine Club CAI, with red/white paint stripes and an identifying number in black. Where this is not present, alternate marks are used, explained in the route description. Waymarking is placed at regular intervals on permanent features of the landscape such as rocks, though tree trunks are also used. Junctions are usually marked by signposts. In addition you will occasionally spot a black or red triangle with the GEA logo. Moreover a series of handy green marker columns is being erected at key junctions; these bear route timings and destinations, but always take the timings with a generous pinch of salt as they tend towards inaccurate to say the least, if not outright wrong in many places. Unfortunately they never tell you where you are. However, they are reassuring and where relevant usually show the GEA.

Dos and don'ts

Don't underestimate the Apennines. In the first case, don't treat them as a younger sibling of the Alps: there is surprisingly dramatic high-level terrain, but a refreshing lack of summer crowds. Secondly, while altitudes are considerably lower than the Alps, the weather can be fierce. Be aware that the Apennines are prone to surprising extremes of weather, so don't be caught out unprepared. Take weather forecasts seriously and beware any signs of an impending thunderstorm if on a ridge route; use the closest escape route to reach lower, more sheltered, altitudes. Incredibly thick fog can roll in at a moment's notice, obscuring waymarking and transforming a simple path into a high-risk exercise in orienteering. Extremely high winds gusting well over 100kph are not uncommon. If encountered, you must keep away from exposed crest routes at all cost and either take a rest day or find a lower level route. If caught out unexpectedly, the recommended technique is to take off your rucksack and lie flat on the ground. As W.C.Bryant (1835) wrote of the Apennines 'there the winds no barrier know'!

Read the walk description carefully before setting out, and if necessary be prepared to modify your plans to match your state of fitness or fatigue. The Trek is not intended as a marathon route. Plan on reaching your destination in daylight to allow for unforeseen circumstances and give yourself time to recover and make ready for the following day. If in a group, calculate the pace according to the slowest member.

Never set out on your own even if you have considerable experience of mountain paths; always tell someone your destination and estimated time of arrival in advance.

Never continue on the trail for more than 5–10 minutes without checking for red/white route waymarking. If you can't see any, return to the last mark and search from there. A felled tree or new spring growth may have caused the problem.

Be considerate when choosing your stop when nature calls: don't ever leave unsightly toilet paper or tissues lying around, and avoid watercourses. Don't be tempted by rock overhangs or caves, and remember that isolated huts serve as essential shelter for shepherds (and walkers!) in inclement weather.

British walkers will need no reminding that all stock gates should be closed promptly and securely.

English is not widely spoken, but the friendly people always try to help outsiders. Do make an effort to memorise at least basic greetings such as *Buon giorno* (Good morning) and *Buona sera* (Good evening), *Arrivederci* (Goodbye) and *Grazie* (Thank you).

EMERGENCIES

It is essential to have some form of health insurance. Thanks to reciprocal agreements, members of EU countries, with the addition of Australia, only need the E111 form (available at most post offices) for hospital care, while all other nationalities need separate cover. Travel insurance is always a good idea on top of that, and the small print should be checked for helicopter rescue. Members of recognised alpine clubs are usually covered.

Italy's all-encompassing emergency phone number is 112. Ambulance (*ambulanza*) and mountain rescue (*soccorso alpino*) can be contacted on 118. Forest fires (*incendi boschivi*) should be reported on 1515.

Carrying a mobile phone is not necessarily a safety measure as reception is not guaranteed in the mountainous regions, nor many valleys for that matter. A whistle – or torch for night times – can be more valuable for attracting attention and calling for assistance. However, by all means carry a mobile as when they do work they are invaluable for calling for help or coping with unplanned changes in itinerary and practical arrangements.

Should an accident happen, get help as fast as possible. Either phone 118 (ask for *soccorso alpino*, mountain rescue) or use the international rescue signal: the call for help is **SIX** visual or audible signals per minute, to be repeated after a minute's pause. The answer is **THREE** visual or audible signals per minute, to be repeated after a minute's pause. Flash a torch or blow a whistle. Anyone hearing a call for help MUST contact the nearest refuge or police station as soon as possible.

The following arm signals could be useful for communicating at a distance or with a helicopter:

Both arms raised diagonally:

- help needed
- land here
- YES (to pilot's questions)

One arm raised diagonally, one arm down diagonally:

- help not needed

- do not land here
- NO (to pilot's questions)

MAPS

Walking maps – either 1:25,000 or 1:50,000 scale, with details of landscape features, contour lines, road passes and settlements – are an essential aid for walkers on this Trek. The sketch maps provided in this book are only intended as a guide, and due to limitations of space cannot show watercourses and other landmarks essential for orientation and location of exit routes. While Italian walking maps in general leave a lot to be desired in terms of accuracy, a fairly good user-friendly series is published by Selca, as listed below (**www.selca-carto-grafie.it**). Individual maps are also given in the headings for each stage during the route. The odd discrepancy will be found in terms of the route description due to recent rerouting and the lack of map updating.

The Italian for 'walking map' is *carta escursionistica*.

- **Stages 1–4:** Selca 'Valtiberina e Marca Toscana' 1:50,000 (except for the final stretch)
- **Stages 4–8:** Selca 'Parco Nazionale delle Foreste Casentinesi' 1:25,000 (brief off-the-sheet stretch after Chiusi La Verna and only initial part of Stage 8)
- **Stages 5–8:** Selca 'Alto Appennino Forlivese' 1:50,000 Regione Emilia-Romagna/CAI, sheet 9

(missing beginning Stage 5 and
end Stage 8)

(**Stages 7–10** also covered by the
Selca 'Sentieri Montani della
Provincia di Firenze' 1:50,000,
sheet 1)

- **Stages 8–9:** Selca 'Alto Appennino
  Faentino' 1:50,000 Regione
  Emilia-Romagna/CAI, sheet 8
  (except start Stage 8)

- **Stages 9–11:** Selca 'Alto
  Appennino Imolese' 1:50,000
  Regione Emilia-Romagna/CAI,
  sheet 7

- **Stages 12–15:** Selca 'Alto
  Appennino Bolognese' 1:50,000
  Regione Emilia-Romagna/CAI,
  sheet 6 (except beginning
  Stage 12, end Stage 15)

- **Stages 15–17:** Selca 'Alto
  Appennino Modenese' 1:50,000
  Regione Emilia-Romagna/CAI,
  sheet 5

- **Stages 18–21:** Selca 'Alto
  Appennino Reggiano' 1:50,000
  Regione Emilia-Romagna/CAI,
  sheet 4 (except start Stage 18 and
  end Stage 21)

- **Stages 21–23:** Selca 'Alto
  Appennino Parmense Est' 1:50,000
  Regione Emilia-Romagna/CAI,
  sheet 3

Multigraphic 1:25,000 maps also
cover a good part of the Trek and are
widely distributed, but their unclear
graphics and heavy printing style
make them quite difficult to read.

Some of the relevant maps are
available in towns and villages in the
Apennines, as well as the odd local
tourist office. Overseas suppliers
include the Stanfords stores in the UK
(London, Manchester and Bristol
www.stanfords.co.uk). Otherwise maps
can be ordered online from **www.stella-
alpina.com**, which corresponds to
Libreria Stella Alpina at via F.Corridoni
14 B/r, Florence (tel: 055 411688).
Another reputable Italian bookstore is
www.lib);libreriaalamontagna.it, Libreria La
Montagna, Via Sacchi 28 bis, 10128
Torino, (tel: 011 5620024). As a 'last
resort' before embarking on the walk
make a stopover in Bologna and visit the
tiny but well-stocked bookshop Nuova
Libreria Accursio, Via G.Oberdan 29/B,
40126 Bologna (tel: 051 220983), only 10
minutes on foot from the railway station.

WHAT TO TAKE

Packing deserves careful thought and
preparation as inappropriate equipment
can spoil a walking holiday and distract
you – instead of enjoying those marvellous views you'll be miserable with
aching shoulders and blistered feet!
Here's a checklist with suggestions:

- comfortable rucksack; when
  packed pop it on the bathroom
  scales – 10kg is a reasonable cut-
  off point. A supply of plastic bags
  is handy for organising contents

- sturdy walking boots, preferably
  not brand new and with a good
  grip sole and ankle support.
  Sandals or lightweight footwear
  for the evening

- rainproof gear, either a full poncho or jacket, overtrousers and rucksack cover, depending on personal tastes. A lightweight folding umbrella is a godsend for walkers who wear glasses on the trail

- layers of clothing to cope with conditions ranging from biting cold winds through to scorching sun, so T-shirts, short and long trousers, warm fleece and a jacket, as well as a woolly hat and gloves

- sun hat, shades, chapstick and extra-high factor sunblock (remember that the sun's rays become stronger by 10% for every 1000m in ascent)

- toiletries and essential medicines

- water bottle – plastic mineral water bottles widely available in Italy are perfect

- emergency food such as muesli bars, biscuits and chocolate

- walking maps and compass

- whistle for calling for help

- torch or headlamp; don't forget spare batteries

- an altimeter, handy for under-standing weather trends: if a known altitude (such as a refuge) begins to rise, a low-pressure trough may be approaching, a warning to walkers

- trekking poles to ease rucksack weight, aid wonky knees and keep sheep dogs at a safe distance

- sleeping sheet (sleeping-bag liner) and small towel for refuge stays

- gaiters for snow traverses

- first-aid kit

- lightweight binoculars and camera with plenty of film

- supply of euros in cash, and credit card

ACCOMMODATION

The options along the Trek consist of a good string of modest hotels, guest houses and alpine-style refuges, walkers' hostels and even a couple of dormitories and guest rooms adjoining monasteries. These enable walkers to proceed unencumbered by camping gear. In this regard, the only exception is an individual sleeping sheet and towel for the nights spent in the high-altitude huts, mostly encountered on the latter part of the Trek. These marvellous *rifugio* establishments are run for the most part by CAI, the Italian Alpine Club, and are manned by a custodian (*gestore*). Reachable only on foot, they provide dormitory accom-modation with bunk beds, along with all meals, and many also have hot showers. Anyone is welcome to stay in a *rifugio*. *Pernottamento* means 'overnight stay', whereas *cena* is 'dinner' and *prima colazione* 'break-fast'. CAI card holders and members of overseas alpine clubs with reciprocal rights agreements are entitled to discounted rates. A quick note on behaviour: boots should be left in the entrance hall where slippers or flip-flops are usually available for guests;

Rifugio La Calla (Stage 6)

from 10pm to 6am it's 'lights out' and silence. Carry a stash of euros in cash as *rifugi* do not accept credit cards for payment, unlike the majority of hotels and restaurants. Banks and automatic telling machines (ATM) in villages are listed in the walk description.

Even when the *rifugio* itself is closed for business, the majority have a *ricovero invernale* ('winter shelter') always open. It usually has a fireplace and wood, and less commonly bunks.

Posto Tappa is the Italian equivalent of the French invention *gîte d'étape*; several are encountered en route and in theory offer dorm accommodation and cooking facilities. However, walkers are usually told that the premises are unusable and are pointed in the direction of the nearest hotel. A *Foresteria*, on the other hand, refers to guest quarters at a monastery.

Note that many modest hotels at road passes or popular beauty spots

also use the appellation *rifugio*, as do a scattering of privately owned hunters' huts shown on maps. Don't assume that they all provide accommodation – only useful establishments are shown as a black hut on the sketch maps.

In general phone at least one day in advance to book your accommodation, giving yourself time to reroute if necessary. However mid-August is peak holiday time and advance reservation is strongly recommended for hot spots such as Lago Santo Modenese, not to mention the *rifugi* on Saturday evenings in summer as many put up local walking groups. Remember that the majority of the road passes are served by buses, enabling you to detour to a nearby village and hotel if needs be, an added bonus which gives visitors a rare glimpse into farming communities and isolated hamlets with vestiges of traditional life. Unless otherwise indicated, hotels and guest houses listed in the route description are open all year round, although the off-season can be somewhat hit-or-miss in view of the practice of impromptu closures. It's always a good idea to phone ahead in spring or autumn.

Public phones are a common feature of even the remotest village. Often found in the local café, many work on a pay-as-you-speak system so you need to request a line first: *Mi dà la linea per favore*. You'll be charged on the number of *scatti* (units) registered. Others accept prepaid phone cards (few phones take coins these days), best purchased at a tobacconist or news-stand in a town of some size.

When using the phone in Italy don't forget to include the '0' of the area code, even for local calls. The sole exceptions are toll-free numbers beginning with '800' and mobile phones. All attempts at speaking Italian are appreciated. On the phone try *Pronto, vorrei una camera singola/doppia per domani sera* (Hello, I'd like a single/double room for tomorrow night). *Parla inglese?* (Do you speak English?), *Quanto costa?* (How much is it?) and *Grazie* (Thank you) might also come in handy.

To be honest, by far the best way to enjoy this Trek would be to camp, but be warned that it is formally forbidden in the areas designated as parks, national and others. For walkers who prefer the freedom and don't mind the extra weight, the odd discreet pitch shouldn't be a problem,

as long as private property is avoided. Always check where possible – for example some of the huts along the way will suggest a quiet spot. *Campeggio vietato* means 'no camping'. To ask if you can put up your tent, try *Posso montare la mia tenda qui?*

INFORMATION

A complete list follows of Tourist Offices useful for the Trek, and they can also be found at the relevant points in the route description.

Abetone	tel: 0573 60231
Arezzo	tel: 0575 208389
Berceto	tel: 0525 64764
Bibbiena	tel: 0575 593098
Bologna	tel: 051 246541
Castelnuovo di Garfagnana	tel: 0583 641007
Castelnovo ne' Monti	tel: 0522 810430
Faenza	tel: 0546 25231
Forlì	tel: 0543 712435
La Spezia	tel: 0187 770900
Lucca	tel: 0583 919931
Parma	tel: 0521 228152
Pieve Pelago	tel: 0536 71304
Pistoia	tel: 0573 21622
Pontremoli	tel: 0187 833287
Porretta Terme	tel: 0534 22021
Prato	tel: 0574 24112
Reggio Emilia	tel: 0522 451152
Sansepolcro	tel: 0575 740536

Restaurant/hotel at Passo della Futa (Stage 10)

Other useful contacts are the Parco Nazionale delle Foreste Casentinesi tel: 0575 50301 **www.parks.it/parco.nazionale.for.cas entinesi**. The newly established (2001) Parco Nazionale dell'Appennino Tosco-Emiliano incorporates the previous regional Parco del Gigante (**www.parcogigante.it**) and the Parco dei Cento Laghi (**www.parks.it/parco. cento.laghi**) along with several reserves. As yet the headquarters has not been decided on, but the web site **www.parks.it** is a good source of up-to-date information.

Some protected areas – not to mention national parks – are managed by the Italian State Forestry Commission known as the CFS (Corpo Forestale dello Stato), whose highly qualified staff and visitor centres are informative with regard to the forests.

HIGHLIGHTS AND SHORT WALKS

The Trek is well suited for biting off sizeable chunks for consumption as single- or multiple-day walks thanks to the excellent network of public transport that serves the Apennine settlements and passes. To facilitate walkers who don't have 23 days available for the entire Trek, a selection of shorter sections encompassing highlights is outlined here. Each begins and ends at a location served directly by public transport or within reasonable distance.

- **1 day:** Bocca Trabaria–Passo delle Vacche–Montecasale–Sansepolcro (see Stage 1). A stretch of wild wooded ridge is followed by a descent to the peaceful setting of an atmospheric Franciscan monastery. The day concludes at the historic township of Sansepolcro.

- **1 day:** Badia Prataglia–Camaldoli (see Stage 5). Straightforward paths climb through divine woods to a broad ridge, whence a plunge to a landmark historic sanctuary and monastery.
- **1 day:** Passo del Muraglione–Colla della Maestà–Acquacheta–San Benedetto in Alpe (see Stage 8). Restful pathways and easy tracks for a straightforward drop via a lovely wooded valley that boasts attractive and popular waterfalls; plenty of spots for a cooling dip on the lower part of the cascading river. The conclusion is a modest hamlet with memorable food.
- **1–2 days:** Montepiano–Rifugio Pacini–Cantagallo (see Stage 12). Studded with shrines this wander through the vast sea of rolling green hills is a delight in springtime.
- **2 days:** Pracchia–Rifugio Porta Franca–Orsigna (see Stage 14). Lovers of dense forest where deer abound will enjoy this rewarding circuit, enhanced by an overnight stay at a hospitable refuge.
- **2 days:** Pracchia–Lago Scaffaiolo–Abetone (see Stages 14–15). Exhilarating if tiring stretch that negotiates both beautiful wood land then breathtaking open ridges, touching on two key peaks.
- **2 days:** Abetone–Lago Santo Modenese–San Pellegrino in Alpe (see Stages 16–17). Some

panoramic ridge walking, a justifiably popular lake resort and a historic sanctuary as the final destination.

- **2 days:** Prato Spilla–Lago Santo Parmense–Passo della Cisa (see Stages 22–23). Plenty of open ridge with massive sweeps of views, while myriad attractive lakes nestling in cirques provide good excuses for a detour. It takes in one of the best sections of the entire Trek.
- **3 days:** Badia Prataglia–Camaldoli–La Burraia–Passo del Muraglione (see Stages 5–7). A rewarding mini-trek through the Casentino National Park, taking in forests, high peaks and scenic crests, not to mention some good hospitality.
- **3 days:** San Pellegrino in Alpe–Rifugio Battisti–Passo Predarena–Passo del Cerreto (see Stages 18–20). Another unbeatable 'top' section that boasts brilliant views and record bilberry 'orchards'.

Following is a list of the prominent panoramic peaks in the northern Apennines, all included in the Trek or reachable by a brief detour: 1520m Poggio Scali (Stage 6); 1657m Monte Falco (Stage 7); 1945m Corno alle Scale (Stage 14); 1936m Libro Aperto (Stage 15); 1964m Monte Rondinaio (Stage 16); 1780m Cime del Romecchio (Stage 17); 1708m Cima La Nuda (Stage 18); 2120m Monte Cusna

(Stage 18); 1895m Monte La Nuda (Stage 19); 1859m Monte Sillara (Stage 22); 1851m Monte Marmagna (Stage 22); 1830m Monte Orsaro (Stage 23); 1401m Monte Fontanini (Stage 23).

FOOD AND DRINK

Though it stays in Tuscany for the most part, the Trek also takes in corners of the Italian regions of Umbria and Emilia-Romagna, ending up on the edge of Liguria, all renowned for their distinctive and memorable cuisine, a wonderful bonus for visitors.

A good rule is to be adventurous and ask the staff what their specialities are *Che cosa c'è oggi?* (What's on today?). It's inadvisable to skip the *antipasti* (starters) unless you have a particular aversion to *bruschetta*, crunchy bread flavoured with fresh garlic, a drizzle of olive oil and chopped fresh tomatoes. Then there are *crostini*, an unfailingly scrumptious assortment of toasted bread morsels piled with paté, melted goat's cheese, wild mushrooms or olive paste. Don't miss Emilian *crescentine*, also known as *ficattole* by the Tuscans: lightly fried savoury pastry, akin to soft Indian nan bread, served warm with thin slices of ham, salami or local sausage such as *finocchiona*, flavoured with fennel seeds. The famous cured Parma ham is *prosciutto crudo*.

All manner of home-rolled fresh pasta is proudly on offer. One traditional tasty speciality is *tortelli* (similar

Taking it easy at San Pellegrino (Stage 17)

to *ravioli*) *con ripieno di patate* with a potato filling, or stuffed with creamy but light *ricotta* cheese and spinach. They come smothered in tomato or meat sauce (*al pomodoro* or *al ragù* if not *al burro e salvia* (melted butter with a hint of sage). A dish of freshly grated Parmesan cheese, *formaggio grana*, accompanies most pasta dishes. Widespread are *pappardelle al cinghiale*, flat ribbon pasta served with a rich pungent sauce of stewed boar, not to everyone's taste, though a worthy alternative comes with *funghi*, wild mushroom sauce. *Polenta* may be available, a thick corn porridge that goes well with stews. Towards the termination of the Trek in proximity to Tuscany's border with Liguria, you'll encounter *testaroli al pesto,* simple pasta squares prepared from a batter cooked on a griddle, then softened in hot water prior to serving, and accompanied by an aromatic pesto sauce of olive oil, basil, pine nuts and Parmesan cheese.

The country-style soup *minestrone* is a thick flavoursome broth with tons of vegetables, otherwise there's *zuppa di ceci,* chick pea soup, or the traditional home-style Tuscan staple *zuppa di farro* with spelt, a nutty-tasting type of wheat.

Second course is almost exclusively meat. One standard is the renowned *fiorentina,* a mammoth T-bone steak; the locals boast it has to weigh at least one kilo to earn the name! Game (*selvaggina*) is common, plausibly boar (*cinghiale*), pigeon (*piccione*) or tamer rabbit (*coniglio*). Cheeses are concentrated on the amazing range of tangy *pecorino* from sheep, but there are other treats such as rich pungent *formaggio di fosso,* which has been buried in straw and is often served with honey.

Vegetables are usually served as a side dish, *contorno,* and will depend on the season, *verdure di stagione.* An *insalata mista* will get you a mixed salad, olive oil and vinegar brought separately to allow for individual tastes in dressing.

The choice of desserts unfailingly includes *panna cotta,* literally 'cooked cream', and those crisp crunchy *cantucci* almond biscuits ideal with a glass of sweet amber *vin santo.* You can't go wrong with a *crostata* or tart spread with local bilberries (*mirtilli*) or jam. In many areas where harvesting chestnuts was a traditional mainstay for the economy, you find creamy desserts flavoured with *castagne* (chestnuts), cake-like *castagnaccio,* and biscuits.

Apart from essential emergency rations (water, biscuits, chocolate etc), walkers need not weigh themselves down with more than a day's worth of picnic-lunch supplies at a time; even where no shops are encountered, it is normal practice for the *rifugi,* bar/restaurants and guest houses to make up a roll (*panino*) with cheese (*con formaggio*), ham or salami (*prosciutto, salami*). One popular snack typical of the Emilia-Romagna region is the *piadina,* soft home-made flatbread with a filling of ham and cheeses and served grilled (no good for rucksack travel!).

Colazione or breakfast (coffee/tea and bread rolls with butter and jam) is served in all the *rifugi* and most hotels; but if there's the choice it's generally more economical, better and unfailingly more interesting to take it Italian-style at the local café. This can be a frothy *cappuccino* or milkier *café latte* in a glass, with freshly baked pastries or croissants.

On more serious matters, the early Greeks referred to Italy as Oenotria, the 'land of wine'. Ordering *vino della casa* usually results in a drinkable locally produced *rosso* (red) or *bianco* (white). Notable vintages

The expert staff at Rifugio Battisti (Stage 18)

produced in valleys adjacent to the Trek route are worth keeping an eye out for. Sangiovese and Trebbiano come from the Adriatic hinterland, then there's always Chianti – the Trek starts a matter of kilometres away from the homeland of that nectar. The unique red sparkling Lambrusco hails from the district around Modena in Emilia-Romagna, and comes in a *secco* or dry version as well as *amabile*, verging on sweet. At the end of the Trek you can treat yourself to one of the locally grown Val di Magra wines, which include a refreshing *rosato* or rosé. *Birra* or beer is also widely drunk; *alla spina* means 'draught'. On the liquor front, where available try delicious bilberry-based *mirtillino*, often home-made, cloying at times. *Grappa*, the fiery clear aqua-vite spirit, is often a home-brew flavoured with wild herbs or fruit such as sultanas.

30

VEGETATION

The plant life in the Apennines is essentially Mediterranean in nature. Generally speaking the southern domains are characterised by typical Turkey oak and lentisks with spreads of scrubby maquis, gradually replaced by woodlands of beech, pine and chestnut the further north you go. In the areas traversed by the Trek beech is predominant from the 900m mark up to 1500m above sea level, though it can even be found as high as 1700m. This is a guarantee of memorable colours both in spring with a delicate fresh lime green, then a continuum of vivid reds, oranges and yellows in the autumn. A brilliant contrast is provided by the darker plantations of evergreens, silver fir and spruce. The most memorable forests are to be found in the national park of the Casentino, exploited in the 1700s for shipbuilding: trunks with a

Chestnuts in autumn

Walking in autumnal beech wood

minimum girth of 6m and a height of 28m were dragged by teams of oxen to the River Arno and floated via Florence to Pisa to become masts at the arsenal.

Lower down, starting at 400m, are spreading chestnut woods, long cultivated as the mainstay of many an Apennine community for both timber and fruit, once dried and ground into nutritious flour.

In the wake of the ice ages the northernmost regions of the Apennines were 'invaded' by alpine plant types in search of warmer conditions, the spruce and alpenrose being typical examples. Walkers will be surprised at the elevated number of alpine flowers on high altitude meadows and grassy ridges. Burgundy-coloured martagon lilies vie for attention with an amazing range of gentians, from the tiny star-shaped variety through to the fat bulbous classical exemplar and even the more unusual purple gentian, a rich ruby hue. A rarer sight are glorious rich red peonies, while longer-lasting light-blue-purple columbines are another treat on stonier terrain.

Flower buffs will appreciate the delicate endemic rose-pink primrose, which grows on sandstone cliffs in the northern Apennines, and hopefully the less showy but equally rare

Cyclamens love the shelter of woods

Alpine pinks are common in the Apennines

31

Apennine globularia, a creeping plant with pale-blue flowers. Spring walkers will enjoy the colourful spreads of delicate corydalis blooms, wood anemones, perfect posies of primroses, meadows of violets and the unruly-headed tassel hyacinth. May–June is probably the best time for orchid lovers, though it will depend on altitude. There's the relatively common helleborine and early-purple varieties, then the sizeable lady orchid with outspread spotted pink petals resembling a human form, and if you're in luck the exquisite *ophrys* insect orchids.

Bare sticks (alias mezereon or daphne) burst into strongly scented flower in spring, though these are later transformed into bright red poisonous berries. Damp marshy zones often feature fluffy cotton grass alongside pretty butterwort, its Latin name *pinguicula* a derivation of 'greasy, fatty' due to the viscosity of its leaves which act as insect traps. Victims are digested over two days, unwittingly supplying the plant with the nitrogen and phosphorous essential for its growth, and which are hard to find in the boggy ambience where it takes root.

More often than not, the way will be strewn with aromatic herbs – oregano, thyme and wild mint inadvertently crushed by boots scent the air deliciously with pure Mediterranean flavours. Grasslands

Martagon lily

Stunning orange lilies are a treat in summer

Inquisitive goats check out walkers

above the tree line are associated with a well-anchored carpet of woody shrubs, notably juniper and bilberry, which spreads to amazing extensions, to the delight of amateur pickers who use them for topping fruit tarts or flavouring *grappa*.

ANIMAL LIFE

Roe deer and timid fallow deer are numerous all along the Apennine chain and are easy to spot grazing on the edge of woods in the early morning and late afternoon. A rarer sight are the majestic red deer, mostly in the heavily forested Casentino National Park. Originally introduced from Northern Europe in the 1800s in the interests of the game reserve belonging to the Grand-Duke of Tuscany Leopold II, their numbers were boosted in the 1950s and the population, estimated at 900, is now the most substantial in the whole of the Apennines.

A more recent arrival is the marmot which hails from the Alps. Modest colonies can be observed, though restricted to northern regions. A burrowing rodent resembling a beaver, its habitat is high-altitude stony pasture slopes, true to its name derived from the Latin for 'mountain mouse'. The trick in spotting these cuddly comical creatures is to listen out for the piercing shriek of alarm emitted by the sentry on the lookout for eagles, their sole serious enemy. He will be perched in an upright position overseeing the youngsters as they scuttle to safety down the nearest hole. Marmots spend the summer feasting on flowers and grass with the aim of doubling their body weight, in preparation for hibernation around October; they re-emerge in springtime.

Then there is the wild boar, a great nuisance in view of the inordinate damage it wreaks, rooting around in cultivated fields and woodland.

Encounter with free-range horses on Monte Bragalata (Stage 22)

Scratchings, hoofprints and ripped-up undergrowth along with curious mud slides are commonly encountered signs of its presence, though the closest most walkers will get to one is stewed on a plate at dinnertime as, despite their reputation for fierceness, they are notoriously reticent. The thriving modern-day population is the offspring of prolific Eastern European species introduced to supplement the native population for the purposes of hunting, a collective sport practised with unflagging enthusiasm since Roman times. In adherence to a strict calendar – usually in the November–January period – vociferous armed groups tramp hillsides and woods with yapping dogs sniffing out the elusive creatures.

In woodland the eccentric crested porcupine is not uncommon, but

incredibly timid – not to mention nocturnal. You'll find its calling cards in the shape of striking black-and-cream quills on many a pathway, possibly denoting a struggle with a predator. The ancient Romans, ever the epicures, are believed to have brought it over from Africa for its tasty flesh, a great delicacy at banquets along with dormouse.

Anti-social badgers, on the other hand, leave grey tubes of excrement, but in discreet spots, unlike the foxes whose droppings adorn prominent stones. One of the few forest dwellers active in the daytime is the acrobatic squirrel, often caught in mid-flight scrambling up the trunk of a pine. The clearest sign of their presence are well-chewed pine cones together with a shower of red scales at the foot of the trees.

In the wake of centuries-long persecution due to fear and ignorance, combined with increasing pressure by man destroying forests and enlarging settlements and pasture, wolves disappeared completely from view in the 1960s. However, sightings of these magnificent creatures are now regularly reported along the wilder parts of the Apennine chain as the population expands successfully northwards, current studies confirming their safe arrival as far up as the Maritime Alps. Rather smaller than their North American cousins, the Apennine males weigh in around 25–35kg. Their coat is tawny grey in winter with brown-reddish hues in the summer period. They have been afforded official protection as of the 1970s, not only in the realms of the parks and reserves, but it is a rare winter that passes without a newspaper account of a specimen shot dead. Stable groups have been reported since the 1980s, aided by the slight increase in wildlife: wild boar is their favourite prey, though they do not disdain roe deer, sheep and other livestock, for which shepherds receive decent compensation.

Darting lizards such as the eye-catching bright-green variety cause near-heart failure as they scuttle through dry leaves warned off by your passage. At the opposite end of the speed scale is the ambling but unbelievably dramatic fire salamander, prehistoric in appearance and splashed yellow and black. Long believed capable of passing unharmed through fire, it inhabits beech woods and damp habitats, the females laying their eggs in streams. A rare relative is the so-called 'spectacled' salamander, endemic to the Apennines, and recognisable by yellow-orange patches on its head.

Birds include the omnipresent cuckoo, a constant companion, and birds of prey ranging from small hawks and kestrels through to magnificent red kites and buzzards, and even the odd stately pair of golden eagles on rocky open terrain. But the overwhelming majority are the thousands of 'invisible' song birds chirping and whistling overhead as you make your way through the woods that are their home. Early spring is the best time to see them before the trees regain their foliage. In contrast open hillsides are the perfect place to appreciate the skylarks flitting and swooping, their melodious inspirational song sheer delight. On a warm summer's day surprising numbers of house martins and swifts form clouds around high summits, attracted by the insects conveyed upwards by air currents, though their screeching presence is also common in many a village, as they swoop from below eaves and clay-straw nests sheltering their ever-starving youngsters.

Noisy jays and nutcrackers flight between the treetops, sounding the general alarm for other creatures of the woodland. The elusive woodpecker can be heard rat-tat-tatting rather than seen. Huge grey-black jackdaws are common in fields,

Wayside shrine (Stage 12)

while ground-nesting partridges may take flight from open bracken terrain with an outraged loud, clucking, annoyed cry.

At medium altitudes, a post-prandial stroll through light woodland on a balmy summer's evening may well be rewarded with the magical sight of fireflies in the undergrowth.

On sunny terrain, especially in the proximity of abandoned shepherds' huts and farmland, snakes are a common sight preying on small rodents or lizards. The grey-brown smooth snake, green snake and a fast-moving coal-black type are harmless, though the common viper or adder, light grey with diamond markings, can be dangerous if not given time to slither away to safety.

Remember that it will only usually attack if it feels threatened. While not especially numerous, the viper should be taken seriously as a bite can be life-threatening. In the unlikely event that a walker is bitten by a viper (*vipera* in Italian), immobilise the limb with broad bandaging and get medical help as fast as possible – call 118.

A final feasibly negative encounter is with ticks (*zecche* in Italian). While not exactly in plague proportions, they should not be ignored as the very rare specimen may carry life-threatening Lyme's disease. Ticks prefer open areas where scrubby broom and heather grow, so after such a passage check your skin for tiny foreign black spots, an indication they may be gorging themselves on your blood. In any case remove the creature carefully using tweezers – be sure to get the head out – and disinfect the skin. Vaseline or similar can also be used to suffocate the creature, which can then be removed easily. Doctors consulted will usually prescribe a course of antibiotics as a precautionary measure. Another line is to keep an eye on the affected skin for a week and only seek medical advice if any swelling or unusual irritation/itching appears.

BACKGROUND READING

Eric Newby's moving account of his wartime experience *Love and War in the Apennines* (Picador, 1983) paints a fascinating picture of village life during the war years, as well as restoring faith in humankind. Wolfgang von Goethe's *Italian Journey: The Collected Works*, volume 6 (Princeton University Press, 1989), makes several mentions of the Apennines.

Wild-flower enthusiasts will appreciate Christopher Grey-Wilson and Marjorie Blamey's *Alpine Flowers of Britain and Europe* (HarperCollins, 1995) as well as Thomas Schauer and Claus Caspari's *A Field Guide to the Wild Flowers of Britain and Europe* (Collins, 1982). Birdwatchers need go no further than Bruun, Delin and Svensson's excellent *Birds of Britain and Europe* (Hamlyn, 1992).

Indefatigable Giuseppe Garibaldi exhorting the Italians to unite!

ROUTE DESCRIPTION

For those approaching the Grande Escursione Appenninica from the west and Tuscany, the attractive historic township of Sansepolcro makes a launching pad. It is set in the Valtiberina (Tiber valley), a broad alluvial plain girdled by rising waves of thickly wooded hills cleared in patches for concentrations of olives and the odd grapevine. The town ostensibly owes its origin to a chapel built by two 10th-century pilgrims to house a relic from the Holy Sepulchre, but is better known to art lovers as the birthplace of 15th-century Renaissance genius Piero della Francesca. ⓘ tel: 0575 740536, Hotel Orfeo tel: 0575 742061 or Hotel Fiorentino tel: 0575 740350.

To overnight very close to the Trek start you can't beat hospitable Hotel Fonte Abete tel: 0722 80102, in tune with the needs of walkers. Located a mere 2km east of Bocca Trabaria, it has multi-lingual staff and a decent restaurant. The buses that transit via Bocca Trabaria stop right outside the door. To then reach the pass (20min), take the lane on the lower edge of the hotel and follow red/white waymarked turn-offs through muddy fields and woodland.

Enthusiastic start at Bocca Trabaria

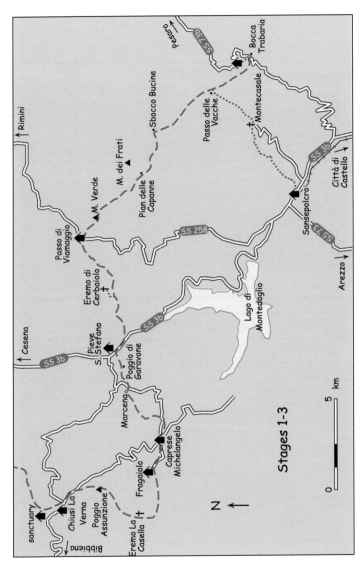

Stages 1-3

0   5 km

N ←

STAGE 1
Bocca Trabaria to Passo di Viamaggio

Time	6hr 30min
Distance	18km/11.2 miles
Ascent/descent	600m/660m
Grade	2
Map	Selca 'Valtiberina e Marca Toscana' 1:50,000

A tiring opening to the Trek, but exhilarating nonetheless. Narrow paths cling to the tight crest dodging trees, the continuous ups and downs a roller-coaster. Dense woodland is traversed in the company of melodious songbirds and masses of wild flowers, with only the occasional viewpoint encountered.

Note: A worthwhile day trip can be made from Bocca Trabaria as far as Passo delle Vacche, then dropping via the interesting variant to Montecasale convent, whence Sansepolcro – a total of 4hr 30min.

Bocca Trabaria (1040m). A historic if minor Apennine pass visited by Garibaldi in 1849. Its curious name literally means 'mouth for trunks', because as early as AD500 huge quantities of fir trees from the dense wild forests along the mountainous crest used to be hauled this way by teams of oxen en route to the River Tiber which rises in the NW. Floated effortlessly to Rome they were used to construct such architectural masterpieces as St Peter's.

Marked regularly in red/white paint stripes and numbered 00 on this stretch, the GEA strikes out due W at first. It encounters grassy clearings and lightly wooded ridge with wild pear and apple trees before beech takes over. Occasional gaps in the vegetation afford glimpses SW to the Valtiberina and its cultivated plain. Veering NNW you climb in fits and starts en route to Poggio i Tre Termini, a corner of Tuscany's boundary with Umbria and the Marche. Close by is

1hr 20min – Passo delle Vacche (1149m) the 'pass of the cows' – though roe deer are the closest you'll find to a bovine amidst the trees; it sports the first of the new-generation green column waymarkers.

Variant via Montecasale to Sansepolcro (3hr 10min): Turn L (SW) on n.4 (old numbering 8), a pretty if narrow path that winds down to traverse a curious zone of bare crests and onion-skin-layered grey marly terrain. Mediterranean plants and scented broom cloak the hillsides. Through a saddle (1000m), keep straight on via poor pasture below Poggio della Rocca. Further down, as the first cypress trees are encountered, n.4 does an elbow-turn R through a gate onto a rough lane. Later, when you encounter a road, go L to nearby **Montecasale** (1hr 30min, 706m), an isolated picturesque Franciscan retreat dating back to the 13th century (*open daily for visits with the exception of a lunchtime break*).

From here you can opt for the quiet straightforward road, otherwise hunt around below the convent for path n.4 W through thick wood to a watercourse leading to the hamlet of San Martino (524m). Torrente Afra is crossed via a bridge then n.4 heads SSW cutting hillsides via the odd house. It eventually joins a road for the short stretch via San Cassiano to the SS3b, where you turn R to the nearby Porta Romana into the walled township of **Sansepolcro** (1hr 40min, 335m).

St Francis amidst autumn colours at Montecasale

Continuing along the main crest punctuated with stone border markers dating back to 1789, path n.00 traverses clearings sweet with broom and passes countless hunters' shacks. Minor pass **Sbocco Bucine** at the foot of Monte Maggiore is reached after a further 1hr 45min. Keep L uphill to a pocket of conifers, followed by several descents and ascents as you bash your way across overgrown hillsides, where waymarking is patchy. Shortly after a signed junction at 1285m, the GEA leaves n.00 and breaks off L on n.8 (W) through oak and beech and plenty of boar scratchings. A felled hillside smothered in broom and asphodels precedes a good farm track, where you turn R (NW) for a 20min leg coasting to

3hr 10min – Pian delle Capanne (1040m). Picnic area and forestry refuge, emergency room open at far end with water and fireplace.

The muddy track climbs past a wind generator and soon reaches farmland dotted with abandoned buildings.

Montecasale retreat

At Pian della Capanne

About 1hr from Pian delle Capanne is a marked saddle (and path turn-off R for Badia Tebalda) – 5min on, keep your eyes skinned for faint path n.00 which breaks off R, indicated by a red/white splash on a tree trunk. A stiff climb ensues due W to **Monte Verde** (1147m) with the reward of superb views over Valtiberina.

Now a narrow path drops diagonally R (N), steep and slippery at first and not well-marked. The gradient eases through wood, following a netted enclosure leading to

2hr – Passo di Viamaggio (983m) which owes its name to the passage of the Roman road Via Maior. It is surrounded by vast rolling emerald-green upland pasture appreciated by sheep and cattle. Snack bar and Hotel Imperatore tel: 0575 799000 doubles as a top-grade restaurant with colossal grilled Florentine steaks and home-made pasta. Year-round bus for Sansepolcro.

STAGE 2

Passo di Viamaggio to Caprese Michelangelo

Time	4hr 30min
Distance	19.2km/11.9 miles
Ascent/descent	505m/830m
Grade	2
Map	Selca 'Valtiberina e Marca Toscana' 1:50,000

At this point the GEA leaves the main Apennine ridge and its 00 marking for a couple of days to embark on a lovely detour. Through woodland and farmland, a charming series of monasteries and villages, hilltops and valleys are encountered en route to the birthplace, albeit coincidental, of the great Renaissance artist Michelangelo.

There are multiple exit points from the route during this stage. Waymarking is patchy in parts, so take extra care.

Leave **Passo di Viamaggio** on the road signed for S.Stefano but turn off L (due W) immediately for relatively new GEA routing via a good unsurfaced track. This curves gently downhill through lush pasture with cows and old oaks and you see through to the reservoir Lago di Montedoglio. Lower down there are enticing glimpses of grey stone buildings perched on a neighbouring hillside, belonging to another monastic retreat, reachable as follows from

1hr – cross and fork for Eremo di Cerbaiolo.

Side trip to Eremo di Cerbaiolo (1hr return time): A recommended detour R up a rough road to the unworldly setting of the humble monastery amidst limestone boulders. Founded in 722 by Benedictines, it was turned over to the Franciscans in 1216, and much later on was restored by the women's branch following the war. A warm welcome is extended to all visitors by the custodian and her boisterous herd of acrobatic goats.

Keep on SW past a Franciscan hostel then a string of rural properties. The lane is sealed in the vicinity of a horse-riding school and soon afterwards a main road, the SS3b, joined. Turn R and a short way along is the modest valley settlement of

50min – Pieve Santo Stefano (431m), the lowest point on the whole of the Trek in terms of altitude. On the Sansepolcro–Fragaiolo bus line, groceries, Hotel Granducato tel: 0575 799026.

Stick to the road through the township following signs for Chiusi La Verna and across the Tiber river (the Tevere in Italian). Immediately after a minor water-course, the Ancione, turn sharp L past workshops to where a narrow road turns steeply up R under the secondary motorway. Pass a dwelling then leave the road (which proceeds through *proprietà privata*) for a faint lane straight up to a house. Here red/white paint splashes waste no time leading up through broom and juniper shrubs to a conifer plantation on **Poggio di Garavone** (708m).

A lane (n.2) proceeds SSW straight over the other side and down to a rural hamlet (Stratino basso, 607m) then a short stretch of tarmac. Keep your eyes peeled for a marked fork R (WNW) for n.20 through to a farm (Casalino) where it's R past dovecotes then L again and through to the road for Marcena (1hr 10min), bus stop for the Pieve S.Stefano–Caprese Michelangelo line.

Continuing W a lane takes you to the nearby property **Marcena** (609m), its fields occupied by grazing llamas! The homestead is detoured L and you are plunged into woodland where several side streams are easily crossed. A veritable tunnel of broom and juniper bushes is followed by grey rock slabs then you emerge at a house and minor road. With views across the valley to Caprese Michelangelo, go L down-hill towards the evocative monastery at Tifi, where a path drops R steeply to cross a concrete footbridge over a minor watercourse. A clear path through walnut trees and fields of maize leads up to a road intersection,

Checking the map at Eremo La Casella (Stage 3)

from where it's a final 1km of tarmac to the prominent knoll of

2hr 40min – Caprese Michelangelo (657m). Bus, groceries, Hotel Buco Michelangelo tel: 0575 793921 and a host of marvellous restaurants. Michelangelo just happened to be born here in 1475 as his father was serving as chief magistrate, though his mother almost didn't make it after a tiring trip on horseback. Their old house (now modest museum) occupies the cypress-clad hilltop.

STAGE 3

Caprese Michelangelo
to Chiusi La Verna

Time	4hr
Distance	13.5km/8.3 miles
Ascent/descent	780m/480m
Grade	1–2
Map	Selca 'Valtiberina e Marca Toscana' 1:50,000

Despite an initial stretch on surfaced if quiet road (bus alternative feasible), a marvellous day is spent climbing through chestnut wood to a ridge with fine views over extensive forests.

From the phone box at the foot of **Caprese Michelangelo**, head NW downhill on the tarmac. There is one signed short cut before the hamlet of **Lama** (516m, bus, food supplies) then you follow n.20 along a road climbing gently in wide curves up to another tranquil hillside village

50min – Fragaiolo (714m). Bus, groceries, Ostello Michelangelo tel: 0575 5792092 open May to Sept, sleeping facilities only.

Just above the square is a signed fork – R for Eremo La Casella. Still surfaced it traverses a quiet residential zone and soon becomes a lane amidst magnificent chestnut trees. With the increase in altitude beech takes over, mingled with pine as you head W, crossing the odd side stream. A good 1hr 20min up, a major ridge belonging to the Alpe di Catenaia is gained. Here n.50 is joined as you turn R (N) for the final climb to superb panoramas at

One significant landmark encountered on this stage of the route is a strikingly simple *eremo* retreat, one of many that hosted St Francis on his peregrinations.

1hr 40min – Eremo La Casella (1263m), where St Francis sojourned on his return to Assisi. Modest evocative pale stone chapel and adjoining accessible premises with fireplace and tables, but no beds or water. Marvellous views in all directions, though these improve on the ensuing stretch.

A rough but clear lane heads due N; ignore turn-offs and stick to n.50 in gentle descent through light cover of oak, beech and chestnut. Ahead due N the famous Franciscan sanctuary of La Verna is soon visible, set on the lower flank of light grey Monte Penna and over-looking the village of Chiusi La Verna, your destination. Views also open up to the E and the main Apennine ridge culminating in Monte dei Frati passed two days back, not to mention the curious fortress-like Sasso di Simone ENE. Finally W below in the Casentino valley are wave upon wave of receding ridges, heavily wooded.

Bearing NE the lane coasts to the foot of Poggio dell'Abete, true to its name 'pine knoll' with a cap of conifers. Keep L but soon afterwards branch R for the faint path leading N via **Poggio Assunzione** (1037m). (**Note:** In low cloud or reduced visibility stick to the lane – only 10min longer and easier to follow. The two join up down-hill.) Meandering across grassland bright with a riot of spring wild flowers and unusual concentrations of dog rose and juniper, follow paint splashes carefully as there is often no path as such.

As the route bears NNW you are plunged downhill through conifers across a track (where the lane variant joins) and finally conclude a knee-jarring descent by crossing Torrente Rassina (780m). Scramble up to the road where you go L, but are quickly pointed R for an old lane. This emerges in a square featuring an aged fountain emblazoned with the Campari logo, a hangover from a 1931 publicity campaign. A matter of minutes either via the signed lane or directly L along the road is

1hr 30min – Chiusi La Verna (954m). Park Visitors' Centre, year-round buses to Bibbiena, groceries, a choice of restaurants and homely guest houses (Da Giovanna

tel: 0575 599275 open April to Oct, Letizia tel: 0575 599020, open April to Oct, Bella Vista tel: 0575 599029). Otherwise proceed with the route to the sanctuary and stay at the hospitable hostel open to pilgrims and non (see next stage).

Partaking of Campari for free at Chiusi La Verna

49

STAGE 4
Chiusi La Verna to Badia Prataglia

Time	7hr
Distance	23.6km/14.6 miles
Ascent/descent	850m/970m
Grade	2
Maps	Selca 'Valtiberina e Marca Toscana' 1:50,000 (except final stretch) + Selca 'Parco Nazionale delle Foreste Casentinesi' 1:25,000 (brief middle off-map stretch)

Within the realms of the Parco Nazionale delle Foreste Casentinesi, this day includes a visit to a memorable photogenic sanctuary set on Monte Penna, which has been likened to a raft of limestone afloat on a sea of clay. The curious name, on the other hand, is derived from the ancient Ligurian language and means simply 'peak'. Thereafter comes a particularly lengthy tiring loop traverse by way of solitary crests and woods, finally descending to a rather nondescript if not gloomy village.

The only feasible alternative to the long loop in the latter part of this stage means catching buses, not necessarily a bad option if you need a rest/shopping day or are interested in visiting historic towns such as Bibbiena on the valley floor.

Leave **Chiusi La Verna** on the paved lane alongside Da Giovanna restaurant. It climbs steadily NNW through pretty woodland brightened with cyclamens up to the impressive gateway entrance to the rock stronghold of

40min – La Verna sanctuary (1129m) founded in 1012 by San Romualdo. Tradition has it that St Francis received the stigmata here on 14 September, 1224. A wander through the lovely premises is recommended and should include a visit to the church for the revered belongings of St Francis as well as the side chapel to admire the 15th-century Della Robbia ceramics, without neglecting the natural gash in the limestone rock where the saint often took rest. The capacious Foresteria tel: 0575 599016 offers meals and lodging on a par with a modest hotel.

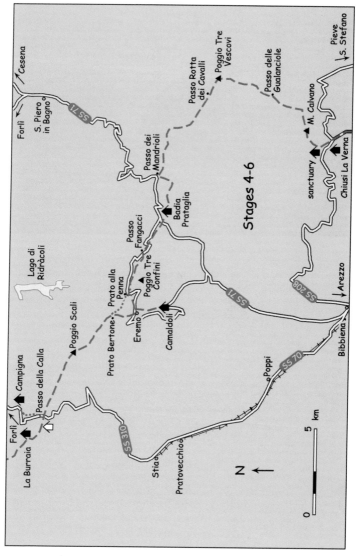

Pilgrim's entrance to the La Verna sanctuary

Continue through the complex of simple stone buildings and through divine beech wood. (If you detoured the sanctuary on n.50 via the outer wall, you'll drop L to join up past the buildings.) After the car parks and a bar/restaurant, at the first major curve in the road, the GEA breaks off L (NE) around the foot of Monte Penna, beneath its towering limestone flanks. From a saddle and cross (Croce della Calla, 1140m), n.50 strikes off E to climb through grass and conifers to **Monte Calvano** (1253m), a favourite with cows and Haflinger horses who like views to enjoy while grazing. Vast outlook E over eroded clay ridges referred to as 'calanche'.

A lane leads down briefly to Passo delle Pratelle (1075m) for a great level stretch with views of the ridges and mounts ahead where the Trek passes. A little further on, the lower side of otherwise undistinguished Monte Castelsavio boasts a spring, a little before a marked junction, **Passo delle Gualanciole** (1040m). Further on n.50 reaches another track intersection and becomes a path heading straight up (N) into the trees – waymarking is not especially abundant here. A steep climb ensues to thickly wooded

2hr 30min – Poggio Tre Vescovi (1232m). One of several 'three bishops' mounts' in the region it sports a green pillar and marks the Trek's reunion with the main Apennine ridge and n.00 route.

NW now, the narrow path drops quickly through beech, marked by faint paint splashes on tree trunks. Myriad other paths fork off in all directions so take care to stick to n.00, which follows the ridge for the most part.

After a considerable descent a lane is joined at another green pillar, but it is difficult along this stretch to know where you are as there is a dearth of distinctive landmarks, despite the evocative names such as Buca del Tesoro, so-named for a 'treasure trove' of Roman coins that came to light there, and Passo Rotta dei Cavalli, once a regular 'horse-riding' route. The direction is essentially N then W through a sequence of beech, conifers, plenty of mud and little in the way of views. The next recognisable landmark is the narrow road pass of

2hr 50min – Passo dei Mandrioli (1173m), the name a reference to herding.

La Verna sanctuary

Gorgeous autumn colours above Badia Prataglia

Turn sharp L away from the road for the steep slippery descent SW that dodges its way through conifer and beech wood and across streams to finally emerge at a sawmill on a surfaced road (812m). For the last leg turn R past rural properties for the final 2.5km to

1hr – Badia Prataglia (835m). Romanesque church, a remnant of a 10th-century Benedictine abbey that gave the township its name. Year-round daily buses to Bibbiena, Park Visitors' Centre, grocery supplies, bakery, restaurants and hotels (quaint Pensione Bellavista tel: 0575 559011, open June to Sept, upmarket Bosco Verde tel: 0575 559017, open March to Oct and Dec, then as a last resort run-down Albergo Giardino tel: 0575 559016. Also Ostello Casanova tel: 0575 559320 open June to Sept).

STAGE 5
Badia Prataglia to Camaldoli

Time	3hr 20min
Distance	9km/5.6 miles
Ascent/descent	530m/560m
Grade	1–2
Maps	Selca 'Parco Nazionale delle Foreste Casentinesi' 1:25,000 or Selca 'Alto Appennino Forlivese' 1:50,000 sheet 9 (initial part off map)

This brief leg climbs back to the ridge then makes its way down to an atmospheric monastic retreat, a highlight of the Trek. This is followed by a further drop through impressive forest to an ancient pharmacy run by monks, along with accommodation.

From the lower part of **Badia Prataglia** alongside Albergo Giardino, take the narrow road NW signed for Vetriceta. Shortly, opposite a house set on a corner, you need the path off R (signed for Capanno). A quick drop across a bridge then it makes its way up the L side of a bare ridge to the road and Il Capanno bar/restaurant, near a camping ground.

Proceed uphill as per signs for Fangacci, crossing a nature trail (Sentiero Natura) in a beautiful beech wood. The road is crossed and at 1122m the GEA branches NW, making use of an old paved way in easy ascent through the trees. It emerges at an unsurfaced road and **Passo Fangacci** (1228m), which means 'muddy pass'.

Turn L for path n.00 that makes its way W on the edge of a dark conifer plantation. The climb is gentle, soon passing the 1350m turn-off for Poggio Tre Confini. Then it's gradually downhill to

If you want to, it is possible to cut the last part of Stage 5 and press on with Stage 6, but watch the timing.

Hermits' cells and daffodils, Eremo di Camaldoli

2hr 10min – Prato alla Penna (1248m), and a minor road pass.

Direct route excluding Camaldoli: If time is tight and circumstances force you to miss Camaldoli, press on NW with track n.00. It slots back into the Trek route approx 2km/40min along the main ridge at Prato Bertone.

Keep L for the lovely half-hour drop on n.74, cutting the road on the final leg to the

30min – Eremo di Camaldoli (1103m). Café, souvenir shop, phone, summer bus from Camaldoli. An intriguing monastic retreat founded in 1012 set amidst magnificent forest, well above its parent monastery in the village. Visiting hours are restricted but at other times you can peek in to see the row of individual cells akin to bungalows.

To continue on down for the village itself, follow the quiet road directly opposite the buildings due S until a signed route on an old track (n.68) plunges through towering firs and becomes a path. Numerous cascading streams and the odd bridge are crossed. Moreover you'll come across a chapel with a stone bearing an imprint of

Cascading stream above Camaldoli

San Romualdo: the founder of the Camaldoli order was at prayer while the devil pushed and shoved him in attempts to draw him into terrible temptations. Not far down you issue from the depths of the forest, pass the post office and reach

40min – Camaldoli (813m) and its rambling monastery and 16th-century pharmacy where all manner of herbal goodies based on time-tested recipes are on sale, the proceeds needed for the upkeep of the community. The Camaldoli order was founded here in the early 1000s as an offshoot of the Benedictines. The land was a gift from a count from Arezzo and the monks have tended the forest faithfully and painstakingly over the ages. The name is believed to derive from campo amabile, the 'pleasant field', the site of the retreat.

Year-round if infrequent buses to Bibbiena, snack bar/restaurants, monastery Foresteria tel: 0575 556013, otherwise Hotel Camaldoli tel: 0575 556019 open mid-June to early Sept, and quirky La Foresta tel: 0575 556015 closed Jan to Feb, with memorable timber flooring. A tame family of boar come scavenging around the restaurants at dusk.

Side trip to the Castagno Miraglia (30min return time): Alongside Pensione La Foresta an unnumbered path leads up into the pine forest to what remains of a chestnut tree. Believed to be in the vicinity of 400 years of age, it was named after the wife of a prominent forestry official. Pretty worse for wear but still miraculously alive in all its gnarled glory.

STAGE 6
Camaldoli to La Burraia

Time	5hr 20min
Distance	13.3km/8.2 miles
Ascent/descent	870m/325m
Grade	1–2
Maps	Selca 'Parco Nazionale delle Foreste Casentinesi' 1:25,000 or Selca 'Alto Appennino Forlivese' 1:50,000 sheet 9

On this memorable day, more time is spent in the magnificent Camaldoli forest of fir and beech, but first off a stiff climb awaits to regain the main ridge. Wide tracks lead on an extended traverse through to a high-sited refuge.

From **Camaldoli** return the same way to the

1hr – Eremo di Camaldoli (1103m) and take the marked lane (n.68) L of the perimeter walls. It climbs steadily amidst silver fir then glorious beech, nearing the crest and rejoining n.00 at **Prato Bertone** (1330m, 50min) where the direct route from Prato alla Penna comes in. Turn L (NW) through a series of grassy clearings in almost imperceptible ascent, in the company of squirrels, noisy jays and fallow deer. Several paths leave the main ridge but you stick to n.00, along the edge of the special nature reserve Sasso Fratino. The next recognisable landmark is the signed detour R for

2hr – Poggio Scali (1520m), an incredibly panoramic knoll overlooking grey clay valleys to the N and extensive forests in all other directions.

A pleasant variant is provided at the day's end by dropping via a delightful track to hotels set in thick forest.

At its foot, where you're back on n.00, is a shrine to the Madonna del Fuoco ('fire'). The crest narrows considerably now with continuous wide-reaching views, though the track is broad and clear at all times. In gradual straightforward descent for the most part, you pass a number of clearings once used by charcoal burners, then it's

1hr 40min – Passo della Calla (1296m). Memorials to World War II partisans, June to Sept bus link with Campigna whence Forlì. Friendly bar/restaurant with delicious home-baked cakes; the owner (tel: 0575 570359) has the keys to cosy unmanned Rifugio La Calla next door. Property of CAI Stia tel: 0575 583966, it has blankets and a kitchen, though the adjacent restaurant will do dinners on request.

Variant to Campigna (1hr 30min return): If needs be, you can always make the detour N down through beautiful forest to a handful of comfortable hotels. After a short stretch of tarmac an atmospheric track breaks off R, revealing lengthy vestiges of the 19th-century paved road, remarkably intact. A lovely cascade precedes **Campigna** (40min, 1077m) *with a Park Visitors' Centre, year-round bus to Forlì and humble Albergo Lo Scoiattolo tel: 0543 980052, run by a talented nature photographer, or marginally pricier Gran Duca tel: 0543 980051, which occupies the former duke's hunting lodge.*

Alongside the restaurant clear path n.00 climbs steadily NW through beech. After a ski lift and old stone building, it emerges on the NE flank of Monte Gabrendo to

40min – La Burraia (1358m), important high-altitude pasture worked until the 1950s and renowned for its 'butter'. Shortly R is stunningly positioned Rifugio CAI di Forlì tel: 0543 980074, sleeps 54, open April to late Sept and some weekends.

STAGE 7
La Burraia to Passo del Muraglione

Time	4hr 30min
Distance	13.4km/8.3 miles
Ascent/descent	470m/920m
Grade	2
Maps	Selca 'Parco Nazionale delle Foreste Casentinesi' 1:25,000 or Selca 'Alto Appennino Forlivese' 1:50,000 sheet 9

An incredibly varied if tiring day over a fascinating variety of terrain. It begins with a gentle climb to Monte Falco then descends through forest to a string of scenic ridges before a final leg coasting in to the pass.

From **La Burraia**, path n.00 crosses open grassland to the crest and follows a lane R (NNW) into beech where red/white waymarking resumes. You are led up a scenic ridge amongst springy dwarf mountain pines alive with songbirds. A military installation is detoured, a ski lift passed, then a stretch due W concludes at a strategic path junction. Here you leave n.00 temporarily to take the L branch for the worthwhile 10min return detour for

Spring walkers should expect some late-lying snow on north-facing flanks during the initial high-altitude section.

1hr – Monte Falco (1657m), the highest mountain in the Park. The summit clearing spells sweeping views. A special reserve has been declared here to protect the myriad rare flora survivors of a long-gone ice age. On the SW flank of neighbouring 1654m Monte Falterona is the source of the Arno river which flows through Florence on its way to the Tyrrhenian. Walkers must not leave the marked paths.

Back at the junction resume n.00 for the constant descent N through wood to an unsurfaced road at Passo Piancancelli (30min, 1500m).

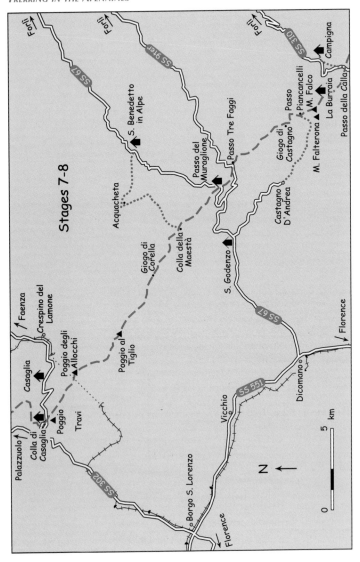

Stages 7-8

Track to Castagno D'Andrea (1hr 40min): A good track n.8 drops L to the village of Castagno D'Andrea (757m), birthplace of another leading Renaissance artist. *Bus to San Godenzo.*

Keep straight over for a pretty path threading its way through dense beech wood. About 10min along at a sort of timber bridge and unsigned fork, keep L downhill for n.00 which winds its way decidedly in descent (essentially N) to emerge on a forestry track amidst conifers. A short way along L will see you at a locked private hut **Rifugio Fontanelle** (45min, 1389m).

A clear path heads W and you're quickly lunging downhill to see the light of day once more on a delightful scenic ridge. Lovely view S to a waterfall and the joint summits of Falterona and Falco, while below is a divine green valley with scattered farms. Not far down n.00 turns L onto a good forestry track and gains open hillside and the broad saddle of

Snow may be encountered early summer during the descent from Monte Falco

1hr 20min – Giogo di Castagno (1082m) *or Cima Giogo. Well-placed bench for enjoying the panorama that takes in the village of San Godenzo WNW.*

Half an hour along on Poggio Piano (1108m) you break L off the track for a leisurely panoramic path NNW through light wood criss-crossed with boar tracks. The Park border is followed then the track rejoined to climb a modest dry rise thick with broom, not far from the minor road and scenic **Passo Tre Faggi** (50min, 930m), the name 'three beeches pass' presumably tongue-in-cheek in view of the abundance of trees!

Now it's NW across fields thick with orchids and into light woodland. A matter of minutes from the pass, keep L at a fork for a pretty scenic stretch across dry terrain with Mediterranean herbs and shrubs, not to mention an infinity of lizards. A couple of slightly exposed passages are encountered, slippery in wet conditions. **Note**: These can be avoided if desired by turning R at the aforementioned fork; timing is similar but it is less panoramic. You finally coast in to

2hr 10min – Passo del Muraglione (907m) so-named for the ponderous elongated masonry wall dating back to the 1830s, designed to prevent carriages from overturning in the strong winds that characterise the Apennines. Incredibly popular with motorcyclists (as you'll discover for yourself if you happen through on a weekend or bank holiday). Couple of bar/restaurants with draught beer and delicious toasted piadine snacks. Hotel Passo Muraglione tel: 055 8374019; should the friendly hotel not be open for business, take either the late afternoon daily bus WSW down to the Tuscan side and San Godenzo (Romanesque abbey, ATM, groceries, bus to Dicomano station and connections to Florence, Albergo Silvano tel: 055 8374043 or Agnoletti tel: 055 8374016) or the minibus N to San Benedetto in Alpe (groceries, bus to Forlì, Albergo Acquacheta tel: 0543 965314 with a creative chef, closed Jan to Feb, or Albergo Alpe tel: 0543 965316. Otherwise Ostello Vignale tel: 0543 965279 with meals). Early morning runs from both sides will deposit you back at the pass the next day.

STAGE 8

Passo del Muraglione to Colla di Casaglia

Time	6hr
Distance	21.5km/13.4 miles
Ascent/descent	540m/530m
Grade	2
Maps	Selca 'Parco Nazionale delle Foreste Casentinesi' 1:25,000 (only initial part with Acquacheta detour) or Selca 'Alto Appennino Forlivese' 1:50,000 sheet 9 + Selca 'Alto Appennino Faentino' 1:50,000 sheet 8

A lengthy leg through lightly wooded terrain where the route meticulously follows narrow crests. There is no respite from the modest ascents and descents, and no intermediate stopovers. It is perfect for lovers of solitude and there are plenty of views over rolling countryside. At day's end, the official GEA drops to the village of Casaglia and a walker's hostel. However the hotel at the higher pass makes it preferable to stick to the ridge route described here.

The route is in common with the main SOFT (Sorgenti di Firenze Trekking) route denoted by yellow waymarking, often more frequent than the red/white splashes. The green marker columns for walkers are also present on this stage, but don't be decieved by the unreliable timing they give.

Behind the hotel at **Passo del Muraglione**, path n.00 leads NW along the wooded ridge thronging with squirrels and brightened by cyclamen. It forms a neat separator between beech and fir, while clearings have been colonised by broom and bracken. Half an hour along a track is encountered and the route does a dog-leg-turn L then R along the ridge. It gradually drops to join a white road briefly, then immediately after the turn-off for Agriturismo Macinelli strikes off uphill through a zone frequented by hunters. The odd over-

Note: The highly recommended 4hr 20min detour (timing from Passo del Muraglione) via the Acquacheta waterfall to San Benedetto in Alpe branches off at Colla della Maestà – see below.

Beech-conifer borderline near Passo del Muraglione

grown stretch needs negotiating then a sunken lane brings you out at

1hr 10min – Colla della Maestà (1009m), column marking an intersection of unsealed roads.

Acquacheta detour (3hr 10min): From Colla della Maestà turn R (NE) along the dirt road. Ignore the fork for isolated S. Maria dell'Eremo and pass a car park to a signed path off R for a lovely scenic ridge route. Some 20min on at 972m, you need to turn sharp L (due N), signed for Acquacheta. This drops decidedly past abandoned buildings and through light wood finally reaching the watercourse. On the opposite bank is a welcome meadow, site of a long-disappeared lake and now popular with picnickers and grumpy cows. It is known as **I Romiti** (1hr 40min, 734m) for the crumbling stones that once belonged to a hermitage where Dante took shelter while in exile.

Keep L of the rise to pick up the *sentiero natura* (with numbered observation posts) in descent for a lovely side waterfall. A fenced lookout is opposite the main **Acquacheta** fall with its 70m drop over slim terraces of arenaceous rock. The unusual appellation is an allusion to 'calm water'. Downstream in this delightful shady valley more attractive cascades and pools beckon tired feet for a cool dip. Keep an eye out for unusual orchids, perfectly at home in the damp conditions. 1hr 30min from I Romiti should see you at modest hospitable **San Benedetto in Alpe** (550m, see end Stage 7 for facilities.)

Continue along the lane n.00 NW at first. You've turned your back on the massive heavily wooded Falterona group now and are heading into more modest and even quieter hilly ranges. In addition to beech woods there are ploughed fields, and pasture and clearings taken over by broom and bracken, the going alternating between ups and downs.

The first useful landmark is a gas pipeline (*metanodotto*) about 1hr from Colla della Maestà. Its access track is used briefly but take care not to miss the resumption of n.00 back in woodland. Not far away is a path junction before a lane is joined at

1hr 10min – Giogo di Corella (1137m), identifiable by its radio mast.

The open hillside studded with orchids gives lovely views over the patchwork of farmland in the fertile Val di Sieve SW. Keep R uphill at the ensuing fork into a hunting area. A saddle and hut (Rifugio Pian dei Laghi) precede a

Crossing the stream at Acquacheta

messy bulldozed logged area where waymarking can be hard to find. The path resumes in ascent through masses of asphodels then ups and downs, culminating in the panoramic top of **Poggio al Tiglio** (1111m), then a junction (turn-off R for Crespino).

Further ahead as you descend a grassy slope, don't miss the sign column pointing you sharp R off the main ridge for a brief tract N. Sunny clearings thick with wild flowers and hawthorn precede another turn-off for Crespino, shortly before the eroded but lovely open pasture crest of

2hr 20min – Poggio degli Allocchi (1019m), 'knoll of the owls'. The distant roar of motorcycle traffic is noticeable at weekends. View N to the village of Casaglia.

Path to Casaglia (1hr): A signed branch (GEA) heads decidedly R downhill to the village of **Casaglia** (754m), *which has a Posto Tappa tel: 055 8402020, dorm accommodation for 10 and the use of a kitchen. The railway station of Crespino del Lamone (on the Florence-Faenza line) is only a matter of kms downhill.*

To rejoin the Trek from Casaglia, head uphill to Monte La Faggetta – at least 1hr – where the description resumes in Stage 9.

Continue NW via a saddle and straight up to a knoll planted with conifers. A final stretch of beech wood leads to a lane junction: red/white waymarks veer L here, but the most direct route takes the white track ahead barred to traffic, cutting through a logging area before dropping to the road pass. (If you are obliged to turn L on the longer route skirting Poggio delle Travi, keep your eyes skinned for 00 after Riseccoli, a group of old houses as it cuts N through woodland, merging with the aforementioned lane on the home run. Allow an extra 20min this way.)

1hr 20min – Colla di Casaglia (913m), not to be confused with Passo della Calla. Locanda della Colla tel: 055 8405013, laid-back guest house run by a friendly well-travelled crew who do memorable crostini and grilled meat, along with packed lunches. In late spring the pass sees the passage of the all-night Florence–Faenza

Lower fall at Acquacheta

69

marathon, known as Il Passatore, to commemorate the best-known of the Apennine bandits, a 19th-century Robin Hood and patriot. As public transport goes buses are rare as hen's teeth, but should you need to exit through traffic is pretty constant for an 8km lift E to Crespino del Lamone, on the Florence–Borgo San Lorenzo–Faenza branch railway line.

STAGE 9
Colla di Casaglia to Badia Moscheta

Time	5hr 45min
Distance	19.3km/12 miles
Ascent/descent	450m/800m
Grade	1–2
Map	Selca 'Alto Appennino Imolese' 1:50,000 sheet 7

This loop detours temporarily off the main Apennine ridge, leading via scenic ridges and concluding with an attractive steep-sided river valley and a delightful converted monastery. Wolves are not unknown in these woods. Walking is leisurely on mostly clear lanes and forestry tracks.

Direct route (4hr): Take the Palazzuolo sul Senio road for 2.5km to a bend where n.00, a clear lane, breaks off WNW. Coasting around the 1000m mark at first, it later drops a little on the northern side of Monte Pratone, and is joined by the GEA as it climbs from Osteto for the final 1hr to Passo del Giogo (see Stage 10).

From **Colla di Casaglia**, head out on the surfaced road for Palazzuolo sul Senio for a couple of minutes until path n.505 takes you climbing steeply R (its signed destination is the renowned ceramic city of Faenza, 16hr away!). At a ridge dark with conifers, it veers R (E then NE) and becomes a clear track through beech wood. Soon after a spring on aptly named **Monte La Faggeta** ('beech wood mount'!), is the link with the GEA path that has climbed from Casaglia. N.505 now climbs to a lovely lookout point and proceeds N through broom and heather, but you part ways further along as it turns decidedly R (E) and

For those in a hurry a faster direct route that misses Badia Moscheta is given – it slots back into the Trek in the early part of Stage 10.

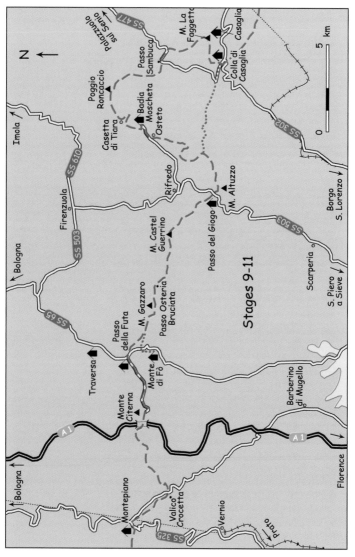

Stages 9-11

the GEA drops to a minor saddle (Passo Ronchi di Berna, 1103m). Here, on the R side of the ridge with vestiges of an old road, you descend gently to a huge cross on the roadside. Within view of impressive grey stratified mountainsides head L up the road beneath Monte Carzolano to nearby

2hr – Passo Sambuca (1080m). Monument to partisans active during World War II.

You need the lane (n.701, not n.601 as shown on maps) on the southern side of the pass. In gradual ascent W it passes a turn-off for Rifugio Bivacco I Diacci and leads to a wonderfully open crest amidst farmland and a key junction with two variants: L via Val di Rovigo is marginally shorter but is less scenic as it follows a deep-cut valley. Your route R (N) sticks to the 4WD track (n.701), cruising high above the wild valley. A good 1hr along the wood begins to thin in the proximity of a photogenic ruined house and GEA waymarking points you L beneath **Poggio Roncaccio**.

A rough farm track dips W below eroding grey terraces past a string of abandoned farms and there are views N to quarries gashed out of mountainsides. Prosperous chestnut plantations announce the proximity of the tiny hamlet of

2hr – Casetta di Tiara (650m) in a world of its own. Cool church, drinking water, scented lilac bushes. Phone and café, not often open.

A narrow path plunges S past a clutch of houses then straight down to the watercourse, old mill and footbridge in pretty Val di Rovigo. Then it's decidedly R (W) along a lane for 10min to a bridge (car park on the opposite bank and road to Firenzuola). Don't cross over but keep on the clear if narrow path (n.713) S along the L bank of the Veccione. Climbing a little through cool woodland it gradually penetrates **Val d'Inferno** ('hell valley'), far from roads and civilisation. Further ahead the valley narrows and you pass high above the cascading torrent that flows deep below towering grey sandstone cliffs, home to birds

The bustling restaurant/bar at Badia Moscheta

of prey. Inviting green pools are accessible at several points for a dip. A final climb leads out to a minor road where L it's a matter of minutes to a well-earned cool beer at

1hr 45min – Badia Moscheta (569m). Justifiably popular at weekends and holidays, but a haven of peace at other times. The abbey, which dates back to 1040 and bears the emblem of St Peter and a porcupine, was home to a religious order that survived until 1784. The recently converted monastery now means a modest museum along with cheap hostel, while more expensive rooms overlook the stream – Agriturismo tel: 055 8144015, closed Jan to Feb; friendly home-style restaurant, horseriding. Bus 3km away at Rifredo on the road to Firenzuola.

STAGE 10
Badia Moscheta to Passo della Futa

Time	7hr 10min
Distance	20.5km/12.7 miles
Ascent/descent	820m/490m
Grade	2
Map	Selca 'Alto Appennino Imolese' 1:50,000 sheet 7

The section after Passo del Giogo is taxing to say the least as the path follows the narrow crest religiously. Each time you puff up to a knoll and start getting your breath back, you are immediately required to head straight down the other side in a knee-testing drop! The latter part of the day is more straightforward, though lengthy. Walking is on a mix of narrow paths and easy forestry tracks. The stage concludes at a comfortable hotel. Should accommodation not be available at Passo della Futa, be prepared to detour to Monte di Fò, as explained in the description. Timing is virtually identical.

Leave **Badia Moscheta** past the stables along the road SW. It's only 10min to the branch L for the immaculately kept hamlet of Osteto (583m, café, phone). Uphill an ancient chestnut wood is traversed and the path heads S accompanied by a gurgling stream. Overgrown crumbling dwellings dot the route which climbs in wide curves to emerald fields, and at a fence with a view and marker column, joins the lane and direct route from Colla di Casaglia.

SW now, you wind up to a well-placed bench before returning to shady woodland for a leisurely traverse with sweeping views over patchwork farmland surrounding the township of Firenzuola. (A path branches off to Monte Altuzzo, a key position on the Gothic Line of German defence during the Allied advance up Italy at the end of World War II.)

Note: This is an especially long stage but it can always be split into two – albeit unevenly – by stopping off at Passo del Giogo for the night.

2hr 10min – Passo del Giogo (882m) or Giogo di Scarperia. Bus to Firenzuola or San Piero a Sieve, hotel/restaurant Al Giogo tel: 055 816051.

A track leads to the rear of the buildings – take care not to miss the faint path sharp R climbing N to a great panoramic ridge dominating the Mugello alluvial plain. As the vegetation alternates between beech, fir, oak and hawthorn the narrow path makes its way along the knobbly ridge in relentless ups and downs. Bearing NW there is a particularly steep ascent to **Monte Castel Guerrino** (1hr 30min, 1117m), a rewarding spot with views towards Passo della Futa. N.00 soon becomes a rough track, passing a turn-off for S. Agata. The next useful landmark is an inviting hut with its own meadow, a perfect picnic spot. A couple of minutes at a saddle and 1824 boundary stone, down keep R for

3hr – Passo dell'Osteria Bruciata (920m), huge triangular marker and waymark column. 'Burnt Inn Pass' earned its name in medieval times. Pilgrims would take shelter there, but when guests started to disappear and the innkeeper served meat dishes the next day… the locals put two and two together, ganged up and burnt the premises to the ground.

Go diagonally W down the rough track past an empty stone building (Paracchia, 897m). The GEA routing has been modified here so stick to the muddy lane (n.50) traversing undulating terrain beneath a grey terraced outcrop. Nearly half an hour from the pass fork R (NNW, 919m) climbing through beech once more. Logging in

---

Variant to Monte di Fò (45min): The path descends quickly W through conifer wood. It crosses the road at a cluster of houses, Apparita, then drops via the lane to the R. This emerges on the road mere metres above rather anonymous **Monte di Fò** (764m). *Hotel/restaurant Il Sergente tel: 055 8423053, a favourite with truckers; camping ground tel: 055 8423018 with caravans, a cramped dorm and pricey apartments. Buses as at Passo della Futa.* To re-enter the Trek either take the bus or start up the lane you arrived on and follow the signs N to Passo della Futa.

the wood can make the going muddy and waymarks may be missing so take care. You skirt Monte Gazzaro, finally rejoining the main 00 ridge (1060m) with its concrete poles in another half hour. Vast views include snow-spattered Corno alle Scale in the distance due W. A short way on is the signed fork L for the variant to Monte di Fò.

The poignant German war cemetery at Passo della Futa

Keep straight on, gradually dropping to the surfaced road where you turn R for

2hr – Passo della Futa (903m). An important Apennine road pass linking Florence and Bologna. Buses year-round (except Sun and hols) to Florence, also connections for Bologna. Hotel/restaurant tel: 055 815255, rooms May to Sept only. A further hotel/restaurant is 2.5km N of the pass at Traversa, Iolanda tel: 055 815265.

A stroll uphill from the hotel is a poignant cemetery where over 30,000 German soldiers from the 1939–45 conflict were laid to rest. The largest burial ground of its type on Italian soil, it was inaugurated in 1969 by a volunteer group; additions are constantly being made as grim discoveries come to light in woods and fields. The Gothic Line ran through here and the ridges and hilltops for miles around were cleared of vegetation for defence purposes in view of the advancing Allied forces. The positions fell in September 1944.

STAGE 11
Passo della Futa to Montepiano

Time	3hr 30min
Distance	13.8km/8.6 miles
Ascent/descent	360m/550m
Grade	1–2
Map	Selca 'Alto Appennino Imolese' 1:50,000 sheet 7

Not the most exciting leg of the Trek as you're brought abruptly back to 'civilisation' by the proximity of one of Italy's busiest motorways, the Autostrada del Sole. Moreover the beginning of the walk is unfortunately tarmac but curiously has been closed to normal traffic due to subsidence, so at least it's quiet. Later on good tracks resume through divine woodland en route to a lovely town.

Waymarking leaves a lot to be desired during this stage, so extra vigilance is required at all junctions.

Close to **Passo della Futa**, in the vicinity of the cemetery entrance, is GEA signposting for the surfaced road SW. Some 50min along as the noisy motorway comes into view with its crawling procession of trucks, the road begins to drop in curves with concrete walls – turn R up a gravel lane with faint yellow markings. A derelict house below Monte Citerna is passed and a forestry track intersection (750m) soon reached, directly over one of the tunnels where the motorway burrows beneath the Apennines.

Keep L to a rusty gate then sharp R (W) on path n.00 through shady mixed woodland climbing to 908m. It cuts across to derelict buildings (Rifiletti, 886m) and is joined by the wide forestry track, a marginally longer but more leisurely route from the 750m intersection.

The rumbling of heavy traffic has thankfully faded away behind you now and songbirds take over once more. Ignore turn-offs and keep to n.00, the main track, enjoying the cool conifer and beech woodland where light trickles through in myriad colours. Via Poggio dei Prati, a downhill section, leads to

2hr 40min – Valico Crocetta (817m), a minor road.

Go briefly R then (unless you prefer the road for the remaining 3km to Montepiano) turn sharp L for the gentle climb to a wooded crest where you veer R (N) on n.00 (unlike the Via dei Santuari which continues NE). The faint path meanders through to a radio mast on a knoll, where you turn L down the concrete ramp access track. Not far down at a bend in the track near a gate, you're pointed R for the final leg of path to the peaceful verdant basin that hosts

50min – Montepiano (700m). A stroll L beneath chestnut and lime trees is old-style Hotel Roma tel: 0574 959916, then Margherita tel: 0574 959926 and further on Cà del Sette tel: 0574 959717 in a pretty lakeside setting. Popular with summer holiday-makers and a key centre for the winter boar hunts, as is obvious from the gruesome tusked heads on display. You're hard put to imagine that main Bologna–Florence railway tunnel runs directly beneath Montepiano! ATM, groceries, year-round buses to Vernio for trains to Prato.

Badia di Montepiano portal carving

STAGE 12
Montepiano to Rifugio Pacini

Time	5hr 15min
Distance	16.6 km/10.3 miles
Ascent/descent	760m/460m
Grade	2
Maps	Selca 'Alto Appennino Bolognese' 1:50,000 sheet 6 (except very start on sheet 7)

A divine stage leading through a wonderful never-ending sea of herringbone crests cloaked in thick woodland 'infested' with deer and dotted with evocative wayside shrines and thirst-quenching springs. You're miles away from it all, circling high above the Bisenzio valley that runs down to the textile town of Prato.

Note: Should Rifugio Pacini be closed, consider either pressing on to Cascina di Spedaletto in the following day's stage (having first ascertained whether or not that is open!), otherwise leave the ridge temporarily for the hamlet of Cantagallo and nearby accommodation. Details are given at Passo del Treppio in Stage 13.

Leave the village of **Montepiano** due W on the Badia road, a divine avenue past a small lake and bar/pizzeria. A watercourse is crossed then, in the company of toads, it's up to the tranquil hamlet of **Badia** (10min, phone box, drinking water), which boasts a 12th-century monastery with an exquisite Romanesque portal. The road quickly becomes a lane winding through lovely old beech wood. Bright blue derelict buildings immediately precede a path junction where you fork R (NW) on n.23. The wood thins as you climb to a ridge through clearings covered in orchids and flowering thyme, not to mention the inevitable hunters' hides. A welcome spring, Fonte del Canapale (950m), precedes a hut then a broad white dirt track L. This is the **Alpe di Caverzano** (1008m, 1hr 20min), the summer quarters for dwellers of the eponymous lower village. Well-tended veggie gardens are very much in evidence.

At an attractive shrine and waymark column, the GEA/00 breaks off NW via a lane then path for more ascent to another evocative tabernacle in wood. The edge

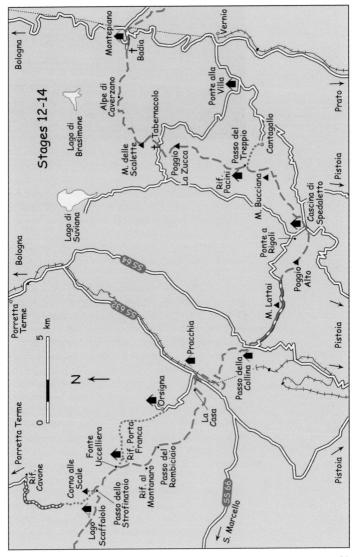

Stages 12-14

81

Rifugio Pacini surrounded by greenery

of the Parco Regionale Laghi di Suviana e Brasimone is followed in the company of old stone markers, to a fork L up to a great lookout. A narrow slightly exposed but brief stretch leads to a saddle on **Monte delle Scalette** (1186m) where you're hard put to pinpoint a settlement in the endless sea of green.

Ahead a further scenic corner dominates the village of Fossato gathered on a narrow ridge, then you plunge S to the minor road pass of

3hr – Tabernacolo (968m) and a huge shrine-cum-chapel. Some thoughtful soul has fitted it out with armchairs to the delight of footsore walkers!

An inevitable stiff but shady climb takes you S to the 1139m mark on **Poggio La Zucca**, but before you have time to enjoy it, the path descends past several path junctions. Further on at Passo delle Pescine, with a moving shrine bearing a colourful ceramic madonna, work of a grateful family in 1948, the GEA does an abrupt swerve R (SW). Minutes after the moss-ridden Fonte di Pluto you cross a surfaced road and follow signs into the wood for the remaining 15min to a superb clearing housing beautifully modernised

2hr 15min – Rifugio Pacini (1001m) at Pian della Rasa, tel: 0574 956030, CAI, sleeps 25, open July to Aug and often weekends. Emergency room always open but no beds. For information contact CAI Prato tel: 0574 22004 (weekdays after 9pm).

STAGE 13
Rifugio Pacini to Pracchia

Time	6hr 30min
Distance	24.2km/15.1 miles
Ascent/descent	355m/720m
Grade	1–2
Map	Selca 'Alto Appennino Bolognese' 1:50,000 sheet 6

After a beautiful wander through more beech woodland, the GEA loses some of its appeal today as there is an inordinate amount of asphalt on the latter leg. The upside is more lovely woodland and little trafficked minor roads.

From **Rifugio Pacini** 10min through wood will see you at **Passo del Treppio** (996m).

Exit to Cantagallo (1hr): From Passo del Treppio n.50 drops steadily ESE in the company of roe deer and scented trees to a brief stretch of road then path down to Cantagallo (572m). *The rural community of 'cock crow', as the name goes, boasts a minuscule café and excellent daily bus service to Vernio. From there you can pick up trains through to Prato then Pistoia for the scenic single-track Pracchia run. Otherwise 4km downhill from Cantagallo is accommodation at Agriturismo Ponte alla Villa tel: 0574 956094/956244.*

Past a number of turn-offs, n.00 continues S, bearing R over a crest and a forestry authority plantation and a spring. You coast S–SW around the east flank of Monte Bucciana, through delightful beech woodland, home to red deer judging by the hoofprints in the mud. About 1hr

Unless you bail out at Passo del Treppio and drop to Cantagallo whence ongoing connections to Pracchia (see exit below), the only way to avoid a lengthy stretch along surfaced roads is to try hitchhiking from Cascina di Sped-aletto S towards Pistoia.

30min along at a shrine, leave n.00 to fork R on n.13. The odd cleared platform once used by charcoal burners is encountered, as is a simple wooden cross marking the grave of a German soldier. Soon you plunge steeply downhill through knee-high leaves to a vast picnic meadow shaded by gigantic beeches and

2hr – Cascina di Spedaletto (881m). Beautifully restructured farmhouse with rooms and meals tel: 0574 933046. The name is derived from a 12th-century hospice. The closest bus is the crack-of-dawn weekdays-only run to Pistoia, that can be picked up from Ponte a Rigoli, 2km via the road NW.

Take the road directly opposite the Cascina, marked n.00 and heading SW. You soon cross a larger road and head uphill on a good forestry track. After 20min of shady ascent n.00 forks abruptly R (NW), with views SW to the sprawling town of Pistoia. It's a steady climb to a wooded crest thick with bilberries and swathes of broom, and inspiring views N into the Limentra valley. After **Poggio Alto** (1093m) and a clearing with huts, a surfaced road is eventually reached near Il Poggione (1hr 15min). Keep straight on (W) over Monte Lattai for a total of 4km or 1hr, in common with the MPT (Montagna Pistoiese Trekking) markings. Soon after you pass a bar/pizzeria (La Baita del Termine), branch R for the last leg downhill to the cluster of old stone houses and pleasant surrounds of

2hr 45min – Passo della Collina (932m). Antica Locanda La Collina tel: 0573 470075 bar/restaurant and groceries, always open, rooms June to Sept only. Daily bus between Pistoia and Porretta Terme.

Take the narrow road signed for Pracchia. Just as the houses finish a fork goes L, as does faded GEA waymarking – **ignore it** and stick to the tarmac straight ahead. (At the time of writing the L branch petered out quickly and the promised track was unusable.) Luckily it soon becomes an unsurfaced track, though the bitumen is destined to return in fits and starts later on. A lengthy level stretch N then W follows fenced enclosures for

training hunting dogs (*addestramento cani da caccia*) on Poggio dei Lagoni. This eventually comes to an end with decisive downhill curves, and past a concrete bunker left-over from World War II. Bearing N you drop to the tranquil green Reno valley. Past a mineral-water bottling plant the road passes beneath the railway line then you turn R along the banks of the trickling river, beneath lilac and horse chestnut trees to

The Reno river is bridged at Pracchia

1hr 45min – Pracchia (635m) in a quiet steep-sided valley, whose sunless depths in winter were once exploited for ice production. Hotel Melini tel: 0573 490026 with spotlessly clean rooms (April to Sept only) and inspirational year-round restaurant, extends a warm welcome to walkers. Posto Tappa tel: 0573 490034 recently converted school, dorm accomm, kitchen. Groceries, ATM and stop on the scenic single-track Pistoia–Porretta Terme railway line, with connections to Bologna.

STAGE 14
Pracchia to Lago Scaffaiolo

Time	6hr 15min
Distance	15.6km/9.7 miles
Ascent/descent	1315m/160m
Grade	2–3
Map	Selca 'Alto Appennino Bolognese' 1:50,000 sheet 6

This stage marks an exciting change in geography and scenery for the Trek. With the increase in altitude, the thickly wooded hillsides of the past weeks are gradually left behind and dramatic bare or 'nude' crests with marvellous far-reaching views become daily occurrences. Conditions verge on alpine in many places with several exposed passages, while steepness is constant. A lengthy but superbly varied haul with plenty of rewarding sweeping views and the first of the 'must-do' Apennine peaks.

The day's load can be split into more manageable sections by overnighting at welcoming Rifugio Porta Franca. Otherwise take the shorter variant via Orsigna – see below.

At the church at **Pracchia** (635m), opposite the grocery store, take the ramp keeping L (E) on Via di Pracchia Alta. At the ensuing car park and communal laundry troughs, proceed ahead uphill on the concreted lane signed n.33. From the house immediately above, take the higher fork for the steepish ascent through woodland of chestnut and pine. Waymarking is a constant now as are boar diggings and tracks, and you are led to a minor road and

30min – La Casa (790m) a sleepy hamlet crowned by productive cherry trees.

Faded waymarks point you up to a shrine at the rear of the houses where the GEA/n.33 goes sharp L (WSW) for unrelenting zigzags to gain the wooded ridge at the 900m mark for the time being. There's only a brief level respite as the path quickly resumes its uphill trend with glimpses of the underlying Orsigna valley, bearing NW through magical wood, a state forest. Apart from several path forks, the first useful landmark – and sign that the bulk of the ascent is behind you now – is a picnic table in a shady clearing (1300m), a good place for deer watching. In the proximity is Pian della Trave, 'plain of the beam', a memory of the timber industry, and an access path to neighbouring Val Maresca, while adjacent is the Puntone dell'Inferno, 'hell point'!

The lovely ensuing stretch (still n.33) entails relatively little climbing, so there's time to enjoy the divine beech trees, grey, tall and straight, and the magical plays of dappling light. Not far on a disused ski lift is passed, then you coast N below Punta della Crina to

2hr 40min – Passo del Rombiciaio (1347m), picnic table and junction for paths leading off to Val d'Orsigna and Val Maresca.

A jeep track (n.3) leads decidedly NW for a winding 200m ascent, still in woodland. A little after a signed detour for a *sorgente* ('spring') is attractive Rifugio al Montanaro (1567m), property of CAI Maresca and rarely open, with the exception of a room equipped with a fireplace.

Path n.3 soon climbs out N to open crest where you follow n.20, cutting along the western flank of Poggio Malandrini, 'knoll of evildoers'. A reward comes soon – great views of dramatic bare but attractive ridges ahead, with nearby pyramidal Monte Gennaio then Corno alle Scale NNW with its horizontal arenaceous stratifications ('scale' or 'steps') and summit cross, and even as far along the main ridge as the distant Libro Aperto, NW and the Abetone pass, all to become familiar tomorrow.

A matter of minutes after Fonte del Cacciatore, keep along the grassy mountainside high over a wild valley to a faint fork (**Passo della Nevaia**) marked by a scant pole and easily overlooked. (**Note:** The 1:50,000 map shows the fork in the wrong position.) Though n.20 does proceed to Passo Cancellino, leave it for n.35 R (NE) to gain the panoramic ridge at

1hr – 1620m junction.

Detour to Rifugio Porta Franca (15min): From the junction take n.35, the old mule track R (NE), that affords marvellous views over the head of Val d'Orsigna to the Apennines of the past days. Just around the corner ensconced in wood is the solar-powered roof of **Rifugio Porta Franca** (1580m) *tel: 0573 490338, CAI, sleeps 40, open 20 July to 31 Aug and Sats May to Oct. Great atmosphere (if no mod cons), run with the help of volunteers, who make sure you're fed well. Emergency room with fireplace always open. Drinking water outside. Info CAI Pistoia tel: 0573 365582 (Tues and Fri evening). As the name suggests, this spot on the border between erstwhile duchies and the papal state marks one of the points where duties levied on goods in transit were collected. A carriageway was even constructed here in the 1500s!*

To re-enter the Trek, take the path behind the building diagonally up to the nearby crest to proceed N on a delightful level path accompanied by scented pinks, bilberries and wild orchids. A short way along is **Fonte dell'Uccelliera** (1686m) where n.00 and the main route are resumed (20min from Rifugio Porta Franca).

Evening shadows over upper Val d'Orsigna

Shorter route via Orsigna (2hr 15min): From Pracchia (635m) a weekday-only bus climbs the 5km up the thickly wooded valley to the village of **Orsigna** (799m, café-cum-grocery store). *(Accommodation can be found 30min walk uphill at the popular family-run restaurant La Selva di Rosita tel: 0573 490094 located on the cool hillside at Casa Sandrella, 950m.)*

Not far past the bus stop path n.5 turns up R, due N. A steady 300m (1hr) climb later it veers NNW lined by old stone slabs and willow trees. Several springs are encountered as the age-old way rises through conifer and beech, where timid boar are often sighted. Stick to n.5 (also n.00 here) as it reaches a broad shady ridge below Monte di Orsigna to move due W along the edge of the Parco Regionale Corno alle Scale, also former boundary of a duchy according to 1791 stone markers. Easy scrambles to openings in the narrow ridge top are rewarded with enticing views to Corno alle Scale ahead.

A signed fork L leads to the sheltered position of **Rifugio Porta Franca**, only minutes below the crest.

To press on for Lago Scaffaiolo, turn L (N) on n.00 along the wonderfully scenic crest studded with wild flowers. Before the shapely form of Monte Gennaio, it drops a little to

20min – Fonte dell'Uccelliera (1686m), featuring a sizeable cross and a copious spring. The path from Rifugio Porta Franca joins up at this point.

With increasingly good views, the delightful path cruises NNW along to a broad pasture crest and rusty signposts denoting **Passo del Cancellino** (1632). You then need to mount a wide shoulder, steadily but not excessively steep, to reach

1hr – Passo dello Strofinatoio (1847m), opening into a vast glacially-formed pasture basin dotted with grazing sheep, its attractiveness marred somewhat by winter ski apparatus. It is dominated by the abrupt point of Cupolino directly above the refuge building visible WNW, while NW is Monte Spigolino, formerly Fulgorino,

Heading towards Passo dello Strofinatoio and Corno alle Scale

as judicious shrines to Jove were erected on its summit in the hope that the god would direct his bolts of lightning there and save the towns!

> **Exit to Rifugio Cavone (45min):** From Passo dello Strofinatoio head NW down into the Piana della Calanchetta trough to the farm buildings, then due N via a road to reach **Rifugio Cavone** *(bar/restaurant) and the summer bus to Porretta Terme and ongoing rail services.*

Side trip to Corno alle Scale (30min return): A must for anyone with the time to spare, it spells brilliant views on a clear, preferably wind-blown day. Myriad wild flowers including alpine asters and gorgeous martagon lilies dot the way. An easy path leads N to the broad 1945m uppermost crest of the sandstone block, and a chair lift. An invaluable orientation table tells you what you should be seeing, SW to the Tyrrhenian Sea and islands, then N across the vast industrial Po plain to the Dolomites and numerous landmark alpine groups, such as glaciated Monte Rosa. Return the same way to Passo dello Strofinatoio.

The final stretch for the day sticks to n.00 and the panoramic crest with a few more minor ups and downs, W for the most part. It transits by way of Passo dei Tre Termini (1785m), erstwhile border between Modena, Tuscany and the Papal State, and cruises over to

45min – Lago Scaffaiolo (1790m), a shallow muddy pond set in a slight depression on the crest dividing Tuscany from Emilia-Romagna. The name derives from 'scaffa', an old term for a natural basin. The unassuming rather drab lake is the subject of murky stories linked to the winds of amazing strength that come driving in unannounced from the west, gusting to the tune of 120km per hour. Locals used to claim that even a pebble cast into the waters would stir up thick mist and unleash mighty storms, a belief immortalised by 14th-century writer Giovanni Boccaccio. Moreover it was long held that the lake was linked to the sea by a hidden channel.

Apart from the hopefully good views, another excellent reason to come is newly inaugurated hospitable Rifugio Duca degli Abruzzi, tel: 0534 53390 or mobile 347 7505007, CAI, sleeps 26, open early to mid-June through to late Sept. It promises hot showers and pasta smothered with rich ragù, the tomatoey-meat sauce that made Bologna famous. An earlier hut occupies the far side of the lake, successor of the earliest Alpine Club refuge in the Apennines, dating back to 1878, named after a great explorer and mountaineer.

STAGE 15
Lago Scaffaiolo to Abetone

Time	6hr
Distance	16.1km/10 miles
Ascent/descent	500m/900m
Grade	3
Maps	Selca 'Alto Appennino Bolognese' 1:50,000 sheet 6 (except end on sheet 5)

An exhilarating – if tiring – walk that meticulously follows the exciting ridge with its razor-thin profile and non-stop views, this takes in numerous peaks before dropping to the mountain resort of Abetone, boasting a magnificent state forest, full range of services and accommodation. The long exposed stretches on the central section necessitate a sure foot and are unsuitable for sufferers of vertigo. A further warning, one echoed by refuge staff: under no circumstances should anyone set out on this leg in uncertain weather, including forecast thunderstorms; moreover, the infamous high winds can blow you off your feet in a trice. Along the way are a series of clearly marked exit paths if needs be.

Apart from waiting out bad weather, the only feasible – though terribly lengthy – variant would be to take the rough road south from Passo Croce Arcana and make your way to the SS12, where transport (bus or hitchhiking) to the Abetone pass is feasible.

Leave **Lago Scaffaiolo** on n.00 striking out NW along the ridge to Passo Calanca. Another ancient pass, it used to be known as Colle dell'Ancisa, a reference to the practice of cutting tree trunks with a view to topple them onto invading Romans. Then take the middle if initially unmarked path on a level around Monte Spigolino and towards a cluster of aerials. Just metres below them is a memorial to events of World War II and

45min – Passo Croce Arcana (1675m), 'arcane cross', a strategic pass between the Po plain and the Tuscan coast back in the time of the Lombard Kingdom, 6–8th century AD. In 1479 it witnessed the passage of 2000 horses and 500 foot soldiers belonging to a Milanese army, and was

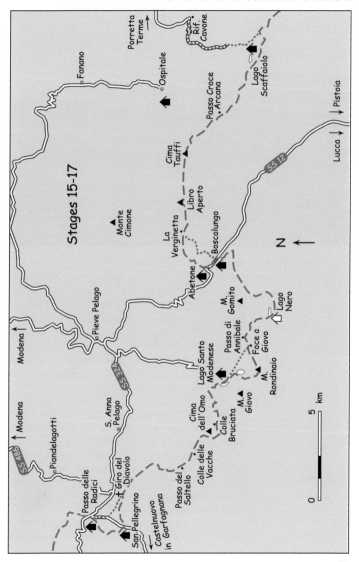

Stages 15-17

N ←

0   5 km

93

En route to Libro Aperto, backed by Monte Cimone

actually paved in 1633. Now a dirt road it leads S, eventually connecting to the SS12, while in the opposite direction (N) it drops in 1hr via Agriturismo Il Feliceto tel: 0536 68409 to Ospitale, though the closest bus is a further 5km away at Fanano (for Modena).

Head straight across the road to climb the next knoll on the rollercoaster n.00 route with historic stone markers. You'll find yourself in the company of gorgeous gentians, curious pink bistort and melodious skylarks, while shy marmots shelter in the valleys a tad below.

The next recognisable landmark is Colle dell'Acqua Marcia (1632m), where a path forks N, destination Ospitale. An uphill slog leads to 1799m **Cima Tauffi**, whose rocky top falls away dramatically with a crumbly near-vertical descent via an exposed shoulder and known by local jokers as the *salto della morte*, 'death leap'! A string of narrow bare crests comes next. The good news is the amazing display of over-sized pale blue columbines hanging precariously off the cliffs, aromatic wild thyme, and even the odd martagon lily. On terrain decidedly alpine in character, a string of minor path junctions are encountered at broader grassbound saddles spread with bilberry shrubs, each a chance to bail out to lower altitudes before the stiff climb. Then due W a good stony path makes its way 300m upwards, with a final northwards stretch for the peak of

3hr 15min – Libro Aperto (1936m). The name 'open book' can be better understood from the northern approach where the arenaceous rock layers give the distinctive appearance of pages. This straightforward and extremely rewarding scenic peak gives onto taller 2165m Monte Cimone due N, with its clutch of aerials. In the latter years of World War II the area witnessed operations by partisan groups paving the way for the Allied advance.

A short backtrack and drop R (SW) is a marked dip and a vantage point for admiring the thick banks of July-blooming alpenrose that adorn the northwestern flank of the mountain. (The path R is a more direct route to La Verginetta.) There's a slight rise adhering to a more scenic ridge for bird's-eye views of the resort and forest

On Cupolino surveying the following day's ridges

at your feet. At last the descent begins, gradually due W, across grassland to the shelter of trees, preceding a modest shrine at **La Verginetta** (1hr, 1500m). Close by is a rustic summertime hut that emanates tempting barbeque aromas.

A jeep track leads off W, plunging into the depths of the Abetone forest of firs for the most part. A matter of minutes on, a path forks L for the direct route to Boscolungo.

Direct route to Boscolungo (1hr): For walkers who don't need the shops and banking facilities at Abetone, head SW in easy descent through magnificent trees, emerging on the SS12, virtually opposite the huge sign at the entrance for the Ostello at **Boscolungo** (1360m).

An easy stroll in imperceptible descent passes a spring and track junction, before proceeding S beneath divine towering trees. Once you've reached the main road, turn L for

2hr – Abetone (1388m). The name itself means 'big fir tree' in memory of a colossal exemplar felled to make way for the road; such was its girth that the outstretched arms of six men were insufficient to circle it completely! Huge twin pyramidal monuments commemorate the inauguration of the Giardini-Ximenes road that launched this mountain resort; it took from 1766 to 1778 to build at a cost of 2,612,895 lire to Tuscany, and 6,412,398 lire to Modena. The Abetone is a renowned winter resort where skiing has been practised since far-off 1904.

ⓘ tel: 0573 60231, heaps of hotels (such as Primula tel: 0573 601008 open mid-June to mid-Sept), shops, ATM, year-round coaches to Pistoia and Modena. The friendly Boscolungo Youth Hostel is 10min/1km down the road in the Pistoia direction; Ostello per la Gioventù tel: 0573 60117, sleeps 100, open year-round. Cheap sleeps and meals.

STAGE 16
Abetone to Lago Santo Modenese

Time	6hr
Distance	15.6km/9.7 miles
Ascent/descent	760m/650m
Grade	2–3 (with easier alternative)
Map	Selca 'Alto Appennino Modenese' 1:50,000 sheet 5

A really lovely day's walk that takes in more inspiring forest, pretty high-altitude lakes and a memorable summit in a pure alpine ambience. It concludes at a renowned lake that despite its popularity has lost none of its charm, and has comfortable guest houses offering a great overnight stay. There's plenty of variety in woodland, open grassland and along crests with masses of wild flowers and berry fruit.

From the **Abetone** pass, take the road down to **Boscolungo**. The road alongside the Ostello (GEA waymarks) quickly enters magnificent forest as a path, with red-spot waymarks at first. A broad forestry track is soon joined (L) climbing gently SSE through an inspiring canopy of beech and silver fir.

After a defunct ski lift and piste, veer R (W) on n.102 at the ensuing junction. An old mule track coasts through a beautiful side valley of beech and vivid laburnums, with the sound of running water far below. Sheer rock outcrops are used by rock climbers, *palestra di roccia*, while circular clearings denote former use by charcoal burners. After another disued ski lift, a broad track is joined for a steeper climb with thinning woodland and clearings crammed with purple orchids. Nearing the valley head, turn off R for the well-marked path n.104 for Lago Nero. A short ascent and you burst onto grassland, a dense carpet of bilberry and juniper. A low rise is all that separates you from a cirque housing

Towards the end of this stage is the climb to the summit of Monte Rondinaio (rating grade 2–3 due to exposure); however, an easier variant is given from Foce a Giovo.

Lago Nero and the bivacco

2hr – Lago Nero (1730m) set amidst glacially smoothed rocks in sight of Monte Gomito. Close by is Bivacco Lagonero, property of CAI Pistoia; sleeps six, no drinking water, open weekends end June to end Aug, tel: 0573 365582 Tues and Fri evening.

Path n.100 climbs high above the lake heading N through masses of wild flowers to a minor pass where views open up W to the ridges in store. Now n.519 leads below the main crest and essentially W across ski pistes and monstrous *roches moutonnées* (so-called for their resemblance to reclining sheep). It reaches a derelict building at evocatively named Passo di Annibale (1798m). Legend has it that the great Carthaginian general Hannibal passed this way en route to defeat the Romans, though other reports have him using Passo Calanca in Stage 15.

A divinely green pasture valley is traversed in slight descent, multitudinous orchids and cotton grass flourishing on marshy patches. The next landmark is

1hr – Foce a Giovo (1674m), a saddle featuring a shrine. The jeep track is the successor of the politically motivated road put through in the early 19th century to link the influential cities of Lucca to the south and Modena to the north, and pointedly detour their powerful rival, Tuscany. The story goes that the Duchess of Lucca and the Duke of Modena – who were betrothed – came face to face for the very first time halfway along the road. On seeing the advanced state and greying hair of her husband-to-be, the Duchess reportedly commented, 'it's snowing in the mountains', to which he promptly responded, 'if it's snowing in the mountains then the cows should go back down to the valley'. The nuptials were called off. . .

To avoid the ensuing moderately exposed climb to Monte Rondinaio, take the easy variant.

> **Easy variant to Lago Santo Modenese (1hr 10min):** Though it's a pity to miss the scenic stretches and aerial views of lakes, from Foce a Giovo a straightforward path n.519 heads downhill R (NW). Following the base of an immense rock ridge, it crosses grassy terrain then woodland. It links up with the main route a short way below Lago Baccio, with only 10min to go for Lago Santo Modenese.

Path n.00 effects a series of gentle ups and downs moving up to the main ridge, high above a string of lakes nestling below an imposing bastion topped with a cross, emanating from Monte Rondinaio. After a path junction (*further alternate descent route on n.517*) a nick-like pass is reached, where the climb starts to become arduous. Exposed and steep but with brilliant views, it scrambles up the southeast shoulder, bright with purple asters, finally gaining superbly panoramic

1hr 30min – Monte Rondinaio (1964m). The highest point on the whole of the Trek with views that take in the marvellous spread of the Garfagnana valley SW with the backdrop of the Alpi Apuane. NE Monte Cimone stands out, and closer at hand is Monte Giovo NW towering over Lago Baccio and its cirque. True to its name, the Rondinaio summit swarms with zooming swifts who evidently frequent these altitudes for the guaranteed supply of clay for their nests, while the bare lower slopes are home to marmots. Beware of lingering late up here, however, as stories circulate of witches' gatherings and scary ghosts appearing in swirling mist.

It's all downhill from here so head via the easy rocky crest for 15min to a minor saddle, Valico del Passetto (1870m), former passage for the via dei remi, 'way of the oars'; trunks from the Abetone forest were hauled this way en route to the Tyrrhenian coast for shipbuilding. At this point you leave n.00 for n.523 down R. Thick juniper shrub cover precedes the welcome shade of beech woodland for the steady drop to lovely Lago Baccio (1554m), which boasts a fascinating range of rushes, fish and naturally popular picnic spots. At the far end of the lake, a well-trodden path drops through a beautiful wood, past the junction for the easy variant from Foce a Giovo. A short cut soon breaks off L marked by red dots, and comes out on the rough access road from the lower car park for

Taking a breather during the climb to Monte Rondinaio

1hr 30min – Lago Santo Modenese (1501m). Out of sight until the last minute, this enchanting lake nestles at the dramatic foot of Monte Giovo. At the most 20m deep, it abounds in trout. The lake's 'santo' denomination may be attributable to the Latin sanctus for 'unspoilt', as it would once have appeared. However the locals are keen to perpetuate a Romeo-and-Juliet-like legend involving two young shepherds from opposing sides of the Apennine ridge, who belonged to families caught up in bitter disputes over logging rights. Once, utterly absorbed in each other, they failed to notice the lake's icy surface and were drowned in an eternal embrace. To this day a mysterious voice from the depths warns newcomers not to venture into the waters 'sanctified' by their love. Swim or paddle at your own risk...

Three friendly guest houses are set tastefully around the tree-lined lakeside, accessible only on foot. You can expect to feast on trout, hearty pasta dishes and

Rifugio Giovo at Lago Santo Modenese is a popular destination on weekends

Lago Santo Modenese

scrumptious desserts thick with luscious bilberries. Book ahead if planning on coming in Aug: Rifugio Vittoria tel: 0536 71509, sleeps 20; Rifugio Marchetti tel: 0536 71253, sleeps 30; Rifugio Giovo tel: 0536 71556, sleeps 30, open Easter to mid-Oct, then weekends to beg Nov. In July to Aug a bus comes as far as the car park minutes below; it departs from Pieve Pelago ① tel: 0536 71304, itself served year-round by daily buses from Modena.

STAGE 17
Lago Santo Modenese to San Pellegrino

Time	5hr
Distance	14.1km/8.8 miles
Ascent/descent	380m/355m
Grade	2–3
Map	Selca 'Alto Appennino Modenese' 1:50,000 sheet 5

A wonderful day's wandering with plenty of panoramic crest studded with wild flowers, and memorable views over the Garfagnana valley and the Alpi Apuane, renowned for the quarries that provided Italian artists such as Michelangelo with top-grade marble for their masterpieces. The only difficulty may be encountered on the short moderately exposed tract on the approach to Cime di Romecchio in the central section, but nothing of consequence in good weather. You stay overnight in a well-sited historic village, one of the highest in the northern Apennines.

From **Lago Santo Modenese** take the lane that runs NW behind the refuges, becoming path n.529 high above the end of the lake. Ignore turn-offs and continue through the last of the beech woods past a spring and marshy saddle to a rise and **Passo Boccaia** (1574m). Stretching out NW is the line-up of forthcoming crests. Branch L (due W) still on n.529, for the gentle climb across natural sandstone paving past a ruined shepherd's hut to incredibly scenic

1hr – Colle Bruciata (1685m), 'burnt col', looking out to the sparkling distant Tyrrhenian if you're lucky, not to mention the Po plain NE. The pass is a favourite with autumn hunters.

N.00 leads W cutting the flanks of rough Cima dell'Omo, popular with herds of inquisitive goats. A length of chain fixed none-too-securely to the crumbling

Note: The route can be shortened marginally if you bypass San Pellegrino and go directly to Passo delle Radici – see direct route at start of Stage 18.

Clean-cut vegetation and the bare crests of Cime di Romecchio

mountainside is encountered, before you round a marvellously panoramic corner (Barre di Tito), looking out to the Alpi Apuane. Not far along, just before you reach trees, turn R at a faint fork to coast back towards the main ridge. A bare slope of loose terrain is negotiated in ascent (take extra care in the wet), amidst aromatic thyme and pinks. Back on top, increasingly narrow and fairly exposed, the path proceeds for the cairn on prominent **Cime di Romecchio** (1786m). Marvellous. The day's destination, the village of San Pellegrino, should be visible, along with the more distant Monte Cusna, a landmark peak for the northern Apennines.

A steep drop is followed by a level path between silver fir and beech to minor pass **Colle delle Vacche** (1700m), where a rough lane drops R to S. Anna on the Emilian side while L spells an exit to Barga in Tuscany.

Continue straight ahead for n.00 via a series of knolls marked with poles in and out of beech woodland to

2hr – Passo del Saltello (1681m), stone cross and dirt road.

Ignore the n.00 signs (all initially promising tracks peter out) and instead embark on the R uppermost dirt track through the muddy wood. At a bend 10min on, signed path n.00 breaks off R for a climb NNE to views of patchwork fields around S. Anna Pelago. Further on, having descended a little to the foot of a grass-ridden knoll (Monte Spicchio), the path widens into a pleasant track. An unsurfaced road is touched on (feasible slightly shorter alternative which avoids the final ups and downs) but n.00 sticks tenaciously to the overgrown ridge. The two join up once and for all near a shrine and

1hr 40min – Giro del Diavolo (1659m), the 'devil's circle'.

Direct route to Passo delle Radici (30min): From **Giro del Diavolo** with continuing glorious views the track heads along the ridge to Bocca dei Fornelli (1630m), whence the road R (N) for the remaining 1.5km to **Passo delle Radici**.

At the marker column, take the easy path in steady descent through woodland bearing W to the slate roofs of

20min – San Pellegrino (1524m). Home to a grand total of 15 permanent inhabitants, it is also the site of an ancient hospice. Purportedly founded by San Pellegrino, son of a Scottish king (whose embalmed body reposes in the church) it offered shelter to pilgrims and traders alike in the early Middle Ages. It now hosts a Museo Etnografico, a fascinating assortment of 5000 household and farm objects, such as rakes for gathering bilberries and ingenious wooden mouse traps. Shelley is remembered here as the mountains and sky inspired him to write *The Witch of Atlas* in 1820.

Snack bar, specialist food shops (no general groceries), July to Aug weekdays-only bus from Castelnuovo in Garfagnana and the train line, and a single daily run during school term (except Suns and hols). Two comfortable, moderately-priced hotels, with

The ancient hospice and sanctuary at San Pellegrino

excellent restaurants that specialise in mouth-watering home-made tortelli pasta enveloping fresh ricotta and vegetables. Hotel L'Appennino tel: 0583 649069 and L'Alpino tel: 0583 649068.

STAGE 18
San Pellegrino to Rifugio Battisti

Time	4hr 40min
Distance	16km/9.9 miles
Ascent/descent	630m/385m
Grade	2
Maps	Selca 'Alto Appennino Reggiano' 1:50,000 sheet 4 +
	Selca 'Alto Appennino Modense 1:50,000 sheet 5

After an uninteresting start, the Trek enters the realms of the new Parco Nazionale Appennino Tosco-Emiliano and is immersed in beech woods alternating with wonderfully scenic grassbound crests ablaze with brilliant wild flowers in summer. With no special difficulty, there is plenty of time for enjoying the surrounds. A warm welcome awaits at the destination refuge, not to mention great food. As the stage is relatively short, fit walkers could always press on with Stage 19.

In the uphill part of **San Pellegrino** turn L onto a lane, as per yellow signposting for the GT (Garfagnana Trekking). Through woods rife with roe deer, 15min along it passes Casa Alpina Pradaccia then swings L through meadows to pass a slate-roofed farm. Not far you branch R (waymark column) for a muddy forestry track which narrows to a path following power lines. At a disused ski piste it climbs R to emerge at the road pass

Note: At the start, Passo delle Radici can be reached faster by taking the 3km road from San Pellegrino.

50min – Passo delle Radici (1527m). Snack bar and Hotel Lunardi tel: 0583 649071, overpriced rooms but recommended restaurant with generous meals. Buses same as San Pellegrino, otherwise it's 7km NNE by road to Piandelagotti and year-round coach links to Modena.

Here the Trek enters the realms of the massive sprawling Parco Nazionale Appennino Tosco-Emiliano.

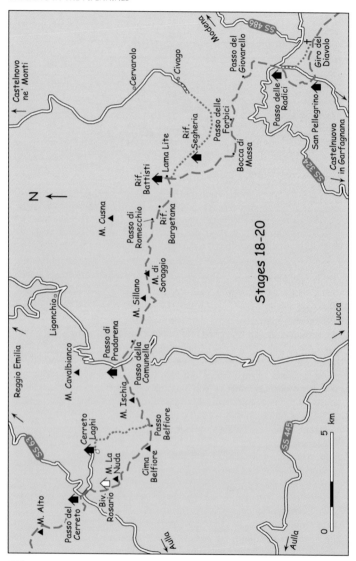

The hotel and Passo delle Radici

Opposite the hotel take the lane N, but 5min along go L (signed for San Geminiano). A short way in, hunt around for the green column marker where the GEA and n.00 turn L through shady beech woodland. Red/white paint splashes quickly become a constant for the clear path wending its way NW. A broad open crest is gained (Park signs) thick with flowers, leading to **Cima La Nuda** (1708m), a superb lookout to the Po plain and the mighty Alpi Apuane in the opposite direction. A brief drop and you reach **Passo del Giovarello** (1663m) and a cross.

Take the lane L of the ridge down to

1hr 30min – Passo delle Forbici (1578m), 'pass of the scissors', features a tabernacle and commemorative plaque to a group of partisans – including a Russian – massacred in 1944 as World War II was drawing to a close. A 13th-century hospice once stood nearby to testify to the passage of pilgrims.

The lane continues to the L but just around the bend take care not to miss the faint path off R through a raspberry thicket and wood for a steady climb to bare crests with stunning views. For starters, ahead distant NW is light grey

Monte Cusna, and to its L directly over the saddle (and out-of-sight refuge), is proud Monte Prado, the highest in Tuscany at 2054m. Below is the Lama valley cloaked in dense forest and run through by a string of watercourses.

A glorious stretch of easy walking around the mountainous valley rim touching on two 1800+m knobs, traverses a thick carpet of bilberries, purportedly the most extensive and productive in the whole of the Apennines!

50min – Bocca di Massa (1800m), a stony windswept pass with a column marker. Bear R (N) on n.633 for the gentle descent into the Valle dei Porci, where you can make a 'pig' of yourself in a veritable sea of wild berries. A series of dips and rises via streams flanked with marsh marigolds as you round the ample base of Sassofratto, and you finally swing uphill through blazes of summer flowers, rare exemplars and exotic specimens such as the orange lilies, tended by frantic bees and butterflies.

Next is the 1781m saddle **Lama Lite**, called 'lite' for the drawn-out 'arguments' between inhabitants of the Garfagnana and Reggiano people in the past. Helpful photo maps of the surrounding Parco del Gigante. Take the signed jeep track circling the knoll N to alpine-style

A well-earned beer at Rifugio Battisti with Monte Cusna as backdrop

1hr 30min – Rifugio Battisti (1771m). Friendly hut run by an imaginative cook who does wonderful things with bilberries and tarts, tel: 0522 897497 or mobile 349 8382733, CAI, sleeps 27, open mid-June to mid-Sept. Winter room with eight bunk beds and blankets always open. Shaded by audacious beech which grows well over the normally quoted height, the refuge is a perfect base for 'scaling' the rewarding 2120m peak of Monte Cusna. A lovely legend explains the presence of this bulky mountain as the reclining body of a kind-hearted giant sheltering flocks from the fury of the winds, and even lending his eyes for the fount of a refreshing spring!

Rifugio Battisti against a threatening sky

Exit route to Civago (1hr 30min): Apart from the straightforward jeep track that drops to the village, a lovely route (n.605) from Lama Lite pass heads SE via a stream and through the magnificent Abetina Reale, forest of firs planted in the 1800s during the reign of Francesco IV d'Este. At 1410m is privately-run Rifugio Segheria *tel: 0522 807222, sleeps 45, open June to Sept and weekends rest of year*. From here on the Torrente Dolo is crossed twice as the path curves NE with a series of ups and downs, terminating at **Civago** (1011m), *shops and year-round if infrequent buses via Castelnovo ne' Monti to Reggio Emilia and the train line.*

111

STAGE 19
Rifugio Battisti to Passo di Pradarena

Time	3hr 40min
Distance	12.5km/7.8 miles
Ascent/descent	290m/470m
Grade	2–3
Map	Selca 'Alto Appennino Reggiano' 1:50,000 sheet 4

This relatively short but enjoyable stage entails the 'usual' wide-ranging views, especially exciting to the Alpi Apuane SW and the rolling hills that peter out on the Po plain NE. There's but one narrow grade 3 tract – best avoided in adverse weather – while the remaining paths rate a straightforward grade 2.

Today's stage ends at a quiet road pass and a recommended hotel with all mod cons. Fit walkers could press on with Stage 20.

From **Rifugio Battisti**, return to **Lama Lite** (1781m) and turn R on the gravel track (n.635). It runs high above curious eroded calanche clay ridges created by Torrente Ozola, whose impetuous flow is harvested further downstream at a hydroelectric plant. Keep an eye and ear out for the marmots which have colonised the higher slopes. Some half an hour on, n.633 branches off L, passing to the rear of private Rifugio Bargetana (drinking water, 1740m). It coasts through woodland with lovely views across N to imposing Monte Cusna towering over a sea of trees. With the odd up and down, you are led WNW to the ridge at

1hr 10min – Passo di Romecchio (1625m), a marvellous outlook for the Alpi Apuane as well as curious Pietra di Bismantova N, 'like the profile of a whale rising from the sea, its head a huge, vertical cliff' for Eric Newby.

N.00 turns R past a shrine to San Bartolomeo and across apparently bare terrain, but home to myriad

Le Porraie saddle

blooms on closer inspection. Tall grass occasionally obscures the path but red/white paint splashes recur at regular intervals. The next reference point half an hour on is **Le Porraie** (1786m) pass amidst a sea of green waving grass (n.639 drops R, a straightforward alternate but longer route to Passo di Pradarena).

Keep L towards a series of fairly exposed narrow passages above eroded terrain. Having surveyed a beautiful pasture valley that drops to the settlement of Ligonchio, at **Monte di Soraggio** (1830m) the path moves to the southern side of the ridge to avoid climbing Monte Sillano. A narrow route hugging the grassy slopes, it soon drops to 1650m to join a dirt track R. Mostly NW it proceeds over grassy hillsides shortcutting the track at times.

Broad saddle **Passo della Comunella** (1619m) is followed by an imperceptible climb. Then, as the pass and hotel come into view at the foot of Monte Cavalbianco, a signed path descends L past grazing horses to

2hr 30min – Passo di Pradarena (1579m). One of the earliest known passes to be frequented in the Apennines, it dates back to the 3rd century AD due to the Etruscan

Sunrise at Passo Pradarena

Via Clodia that linked Parma with Lucca. Modern-day visitors have the advantage of a new tastefully decorated hotel with innovative cuisine, excellent value Albergo Carpe Diem tel: 0522 899151.

STAGE 20
Passo di Pradarena to Passo del Cerreto

Time	4hr
Distance	10.8km/6.7 miles
Ascent/descent	450m/780m
Grade	2–3
Map	Selca 'Alto Appennino Reggiano' 1:50,000 sheet 4

Superb walk with the highlight of the 1895m peak Monte La Nuda and some amazing concentrations of wild flowers. A steep tiring descent brings you out at a well-served road pass.

From **Passo di Pradarena** a clear lane moves off WSW through woodland on a level. A quarter of an hour later at an indistinct pass (Passo di Cavarsella), climb off L on n.00. In unrelenting ascent the trees are left behind and you are led out to rich meadows of mountain avens, fruit-loaded shrubs including juniper, and striking pink blooms from the mint family. After a saddle, the path

In the case of low cloud, count on spending longer to locate the crest path.

Above Passo Belfiore

bears L around the southern side of Monte Ischia, amidst masses of cow parsley and daphne. After a brief drop through wood is **Passo Belfiore** (1669m) and a path fork.

Exit to Cerreto Laghi (1hr 15min): Path n.649 drops R for the 1418m resort of Cerreto Laghi – a slightly easier route and valid alternative in case of bad weather. *It has a range of seasonal hotel accommodation and occasional bus to Passo del Cerreto.*

Continue in steady ascent past the Torrione Tre Potenze, the 'three powers tower' (a further reference to historic boundaries), and curve NW passing just under the top of Cima Belfiore 'beautiful flower'. Below R is the thickly wooded valley of the same name with roe deer grazing on the tree line, while screeching swifts will be overhead in summer. In terms of blooms, the range is hard to beat here, with gentians, bistort and orchids, to name but a few.

Soon around the corner Monte La Nuda comes into view, recognisable for its rather unwieldy summit tower. Marmots inhabit the rocky hillside around a grassy neck. You climb through a jumble of fallen rocks on a clear path to a junction (the jeep track straight ahead drops

Bivacco Rosario can only cater for limited numbers

directly via ski lifts to Cerreto Laghi) – turn L for the final 10min winding ascent to

2hr 20min – Monte La Nuda (1895m) and its incongruous derelict tower. Marvellous views range from the last of the Alpi Apuane to the dramatic Valle dell'Inferno at your feet with its Gendarme pinnacle, and the ridges in store tomorrow. Those lucky enough to be here on a clear day can expect to enjoy views N across to the Alps.

Backtrack briefly for the faint marked path R (W) towards the narrow ridge at the head of Valle dell'Inferno to where the path starts its steep knee-jerking plunge NW. Down in a pasture basin a flag points to the presence of cosy **Bivacco Rosario** (1700m), where two people could just about squeeze in. Blankets and firewood, water source nearby.

Ignore turn-offs and stick to n.00 as it drops through the wood once used by charcoal burners. Having reached holiday cabins and an unsurfaced road you soon join asphalt and go L for the final 10min to

1hr 40min – Passo del Cerreto (1246m), named for Turkey oak, probably at a time before forests were being cleared to make way for settlements. Lovely views back up Valle dell'Inferno, not to mention NW to Monte Alto with impressive erosion gullies, covered in Stage 21. Centuries back, lumber from here was crafted into sledges for use in the marble quarries in the adjoining Massa Carrara province. The SS63 is a key road constructed relatively late, in the 1800s. Year-round daily buses both directions, namely NE to Reggio Emilia and the train line, and SW to Aulla, the railway whence the coast and La Spezia. Two rather overpriced establishments have rooms: Albergo Ristorante Alpino tel: 0522 898151; Bed & Breakfast Giannarelli tel: 0522 898201. Both have dormitories for walkers but are reluctant to open them; request *posto tappa* rates. No complaints about the food: rich *zuppa di porcini* (mushroom soup) and luscious pumpkin-stuffed pasta (*con zucca*).

STAGE 21
Passo del Cerreto to Prato Spilla

Time	6hr 20min
Distance	15.3km/9.5 miles
Ascent/descent	1035m/930m
Grade	2
Maps	Selca 'Alto Appennino Reggiano' 1:50,000 sheet 4 +
	Selca 'Alto Appennino Parmense Est' sheet 3

Apart from the initial bit, today the Trek abandons the main ridge (as it becomes a difficult scramble) and keeps to the eastern flank via attractive wild valleys and a string of lakes in glacial landscapes. A series of tiring ups and downs are included, so be warned! Notwithstanding it's a great day.

If it fits in with your schedule, do plan an overnight stay at charming log cabin Rifugio Città di Sarzana. Otherwise the day's destination is a small-scale ski resort that, luckily for walkers, has a functional friendly hotel/restaurant.

Behind the B&B at **Passo del Cerreto,** a well-worn path leads in and out of woodland, in common with a *sentiero natura* and its numbered poles. It coasts W–NW easily towards Monte Alto, recognisable for its heavily eroded flanks. At a broad saddle you join a dirt track, keeping R, to nearby **Passo dell'Ospedalaccio** (1271m), which took its name from a Benedictine hospice for pilgrims which once occupied the site. At the marker bearing the inscription 'Empire Français IX', turn L on n.00 (also n.671) for an abrupt climb. Not far up, at a waymark column, bear R on n.671 across an erosion channel for a gentler traverse N below Monte Alto. Yesterday's ridge and peaks are clearly visible, along with the northernmost outliers of the Alpi Apuane. A spring is passed then a minor pass gained.

Here the route heads decidedly NW past charcoal burner clearings into a pleasant side valley where the Torrente Secchia rises. The beautiful pasture basin **Prataccio** (1504m), crowned by slanting sandstone strata and home to multitudes of hawks, is traversed via a fire-

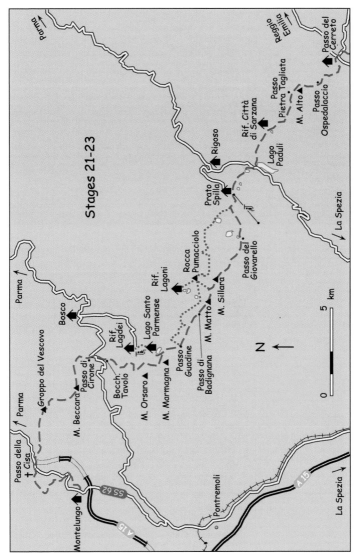

The Prataccio cirque

blackened boulder. (Don't be put off by the sign for *sentiero pericoloso*; it refers to a crest route.) N.671 zigzags steeply NNW to the notch in the rocky crest

1hr 45min – Passo Pietra Tagliata (1753m), 'cut stone pass', high over an attractive desolate valley. To your L is the rugged crest or Groppi di Camporaghena, whilst R the ridge keeps on for the Alpe di Succiso peak.

Clear path n.673 winds down well-consolidated moraine terraces into a partially wooded basin, little-visited but for shy marmots. At the foot of immense rock slabs beneath Punta Buffanaro is the clearing and junction **I Ghiaccioni** (1375m, exit route N to the village of Succiso), where you proceed NW on path n.659. An inevitable steep climb through shady beech woods leads to a fork (Costa del Lago, 1560m). Not that long after-wards, cutting on a level through trees and stony terrain at the base of the eponymous mount, is Lago Acuto, purportedly a rare example of a tarn in a hanging valley, and cosy

1hr 40min – Rifugio Città di Sarzana (1580m). Timber cabin set amidst the woods. No mod cons but delicious dinners in atmospheric lamplight are a regular. Mobile tel: 339 2245117 (leave a message), CAI, sleeps 20, open July to Aug and weekends throughout the year. The enthusiastic young guardians lug supplies up by rucksack.

Pleasant path n.659 leaves this idyllic spot in steady descent through an area known as Quattro Fagge or 'four beeches', better renamed 'thousand bilberries'! The severe point of Monte Malpasso is glimpsed W. Further down is

1hr 15min – Lago Paduli (1153m) and its dam, Diga di Lagastrello.

Shortly down at the roadside in Valle dei Cavalieri ('valley of the knights' from valorous events dating back to the Middle Ages), you cross a bridge L to the main road.

Rifugio Città di Sarzana, a special hideaway in the woods

Exit route to Rigoso (30min): By turning R along this main road, a little over 2km away to the north is the village of **Rigoso** (1134m), *grocery shop. Here you can take the bus to Parma, or if you've missed it, stay at the Ostello tel: 0521 896052.*

Turn L to the signposts announcing the Lunigiana region and start of path n.703a, R uphill again. Lago Squincio is passed, thereafter the way (n.703) heads through woodland W in a steady zigzagging climb via surprising numbers of charcoal burners' clearings. After a 1500m pass on the crest is the inevitable plunge! A short way down is Lago Scuro, which dwindles to a soft waterless mass most summers. A lane takes you on to more substantial **Lago Verdarolo** (1388m), true to its greenish name.

At the western end of this body of water you need the waymarked rough lane that coasts NW to a lovely lookout and shortly a road. A matter of metres uphill past interesting marshes with cotton grass is the not-especially-attractive ski resort of

1hr 40min – Prato Spilla (1351m), which thankfully has a comfortable hotel Rifugio Prato Spilla tel: 0521 890194 with helpful friendly staff and generous dinners. Though modest in alpine terms, this is an important ski resort for the Apennines.

STAGE 22
Prato Spilla to Lago Santo Parmense

Time	5hr 30min
Distance	12.5km/7.7 miles
Ascent/descent	740m/580m
Grade	2–3
Map	Selca 'Alto Appennino Parmense Est' 1:50,000 sheet 3

Arguably the best stage of the whole Trek, this great itinerary ambles at length along more magnificent panoramic crest. It touches on so many delightful lakes set in glacially moulded hanging valleys that you lose count! The conclusion is a divine turquoise tarn with a memorable refuge set on its bank amidst beautiful forest. A fair number of birds of prey frequent the high open uplands, and eagles reportedly nest on remote outcrops. The zone belongs to the appropriately named Parco dei Cento Laghi (Park of the Hundred Lakes), recently incorporated into the new Apennines National Park.

Uphill from the hotel entrance at **Prato Spilla** is the start of red/white marked n.705, a rough track that follows the ski slope SSW. To avoid a steeper section it ducks L under the chair lift then returns to the grassy piste. Not far up make sure you branch R at a track junction, the same again shortly under a ski lift. A path now, it leads over a couple of streams and into woodland featuring bilberry shrubs and marshy zones, pretty with cotton grass. You emerge on soft cushiony upland near the rocky base of Monte Torricella, and a great lookout over Lago Verde, backed by shapely Monte Navert. Due W on the main ridge is Monte Bragalata, where you're headed. Glacially modelled sandstone slabs are crossed en route to minuscule **Lago Martini** and a decisive turn L (S) for a brief climb to

Do not walk the ridge in high winds or bad weather – a lower recommended variant is given. There's a short moderately exposed stretch prior to Monte Brusa in the latter part.

Lower variant (5hr 45min): From **Prato Spilla** (1311m) n.707 leads NW to Lago Ballano (1325m), and drops a little to cross Rio Lago Verde (1250m). A steady climb on n.711 to 1700m will see you at scenic Rocca Pianaccia (2hr 45min), followed by natural lookout 1600m Rocca Pumacciolo. There's a gentle descent via a series of bogs and Lago Scuro (1hr 20min, 1526m), then it's back up to 1675m Passo Fugicchia. After a rather steep 200m drop to Capanne di Badignana (1475m), you make your way gradually up to the main ridge and **Passo delle Guadine** (1hr 40min, 1687m), for the final 1hr stretch in common with the main trek route.

1hr 15min – Passo del Giovarello (1710m), an arduous pass dominating a wild precipitous valley and the views spread S to where the striking Alpi Apuane rise majestically out of the mist.

N.00 is rejoined as you move off NW to ascend the bare 1835m hump that goes by the name of **Monte Bragalata**. (**Note:** By all means detour the actual top on the clear path that breaks off R [NW] skirting the mount, saving metres and time and rejoining the main path prior to Passo Compione.) Improving views take in the promising procession of ridges snaking ahead, along with

The Sillara lakes

the sizeable Lunigiana region and the Pontremoli valley running inland from the La Spezia and the Tyrrhenian coast. The opposite direction, inland, means the pretty Laghi di Compione then modest reliefs declining away gradually to the flat Po plain.

An easy descent brings you to **Passo di Compione** (1794m), and a path junction. Subsequently there's an amazingly scenic ridge stretch above the beautiful Laghi di Sillara occupying a broad shelf as the mountain slopes valleywards. (A sorely tempting detour, though be aware that you've still many hours to go.) A short climb away is

1hr – Monte Sillara (1859m), an exhilarating spot, it sports a madonna and a name plaque and offers fascinating views onto a contorted stratified ridge. The name, of ancient Ligurian origin, may refer to the near-vertical formation.

Across dry slopes colonised by noisy crickets, you pass **Monte Paitino** (1817m) close to some impressive rock needles. A slight drop to a key path junction at 1775m.

Exit to Rifugio Lagoni (1hr): A path heads N for **Rifugio Lagoni** at 1342m, *tel: 0521 889118 open June to Sept and weekends rest of the year. The denomination 'large lakes' pertains to the twin bodies of water in the vicinity.* From there an unsurfaced road runs 5km NW to join the road that drops to Bosco. **Note:** Several more paths branch down to the *rifugio* from points along the main ridge.

Fork L (W) for the snaking, increasingly narrow path via ledges at times. Several paths drop R downhill via Lago del Bicchiere ('lake of the drinking glass') and other destinations, but you stick to n.00 for the rocky promontory of **Monte Matto** (1837m), marked by a cross and, of course, more views. Another name of ancient Ligurian origin, it is believed to signify 'heap of stones' and not 'crazy' as the Italian word would seem to imply. A surprisingly abrupt drop of 150m follows, to

1hr 15min – Passo di Badignana (1680m) and more links for Rifugio Lagoni.

Keep straight on amidst gentians and orchids, high above the vast valley dominated by Monte Scala. The inevitable climb follows as the path negotiates a narrow, moderately exposed crest edged by audacious beech trees that have crept up from the northern side. This means welcome patches of shade as the path dips into the wood. A stiff scramble to the last noteworthy summit of the day, 1796m Monte Brusa, 'burnt mount'.

The descent NW affords a good look due N of the wild wooded special nature reserve (no unauthorised entry) and Lago Pradaccio, at the foot of towering Rocca Biasca. Close at hand is

1hr – Passo delle Guadine (1687m) and a bunch of sign-posts, where the lower variant becomes one with the main route. It was so-called for its role as a 'passage' in the mountains for a long-distance pilgrim route.

Branch R (NNW) on n.719 across especially rewarding bilberry 'orchards' across to **Sella della Sterpera** (1646m). A gentle drop through conifers passes a derelict hut and later reaches a key junction with n.729, important for Stage 23. For the time being, stick to n.719 (R) for the final 20min descent to the unbelievably blue and inviting lake, which you don't get to see properly until you've all but fallen in the water as it is ringed by thick woodland!

1hr – Lago Santo Parmense (1508m) and superbly set on the western edge, hospitable Rifugio Mariotti tel: 0521 889334, CAI, sleeps 42, open June to Sept, Dec to May weekends; no shower. Don't miss the deliciously substantial pasta al gaudì with sausage and vegetables. The historic building dates back to 1882, one of the earliest refuges in Italy. It acts as the base for the popular (and elementary) ascent of 1851m Monte Marmagna; its unusual denomination is a derivation of 'Mark-man', Germanic 'border dwellers' who settled on its flanks when the Romans left the area. The lake, on the other

Lago Santo Parmense

hand, home to two types of trout, has a surface area of 81.5 sq m and is an astonishing 22.5m deep – a building seven storeys high would disappear in it, as the custodian delights in telling visitors. As is the case for Lago Santo Modenese in Stage 16, in all likelihood 'santo' derives from 'unspoilt' rather than a reference to some long-gone hermit or 'holy' man.

Exit route to Rifugio Lagdei (10–40min): A stroll away from the lakeside is a chair lift (same operating period as Rifugio Mariotti) down to the road. Alternately on foot two clear paths, one panoramic, the other more direct, drop through the wood to the car park and **Rifugio Lagdei** tel: 0521 889353, *open all year – a good accommodation alternative if Rifugio Mariotti is closed*. Path n.725 then leads back up to the main ridge to re-enter the Trek at Bocchetta del Tavolo.

Then it's 6km to the 891m village of **Bosco** (plenty of traffic on weekends for hitch-hiking), *which boasts family-run Albergo Ghirardini tel: 0521 889123, groceries and a daily year-round bus service to Parma.*

STAGE 23
Lago Santo Parmense to Montelungo

Time	6hr 40min
Distance	21.2km/13.1 miles
Ascent/descent	540m/1220m
Grade	2
Map	Selca 'Alto Appennino Parmense Est' 1:50,000 sheet 3

This marvellous concluding stage takes in both beautiful woodland and open terrain home to memorable flora such as peonies and columbines, as well as birds of prey such as eagles and buzzards. Moreover, after Passo di Cirone it affords marvellous non-stop views that take in the enticing distant Alps and the River Magra valley that runs inland from La Spezia on the Tyrrhenian coast. Lengthy stretches follow evocative paved mule tracks dating back to medieval times when they witnessed the passage of pilgrims and traders. One route, the so-called Via del Sale, was set up to smuggle salt (which was heavily taxed). More recently wartime black marketeers trafficking in much-needed goods trod the same routes, as did partisans and escapees such as the author Eric Newby.

The stage is rather long and tiring due to the constant ups and downs, so pace yourself carefully. There are no difficult stretches. Remember that Passo della Cisa can also serve as a suitable conclusion.

From the *rifugio* at **Lago Santo Parmense**, retrace your steps on path n.719/723 along the wooded southwestern shore of the lake then in ascent across smooth sandstone slabs to the key junction (30min) where you branch R (NW) on n.729 (sign for Monte Orsaro). In the company of chaotic squawking nutcrackers, keep R at the ensuing fork then loop past a peat bog bright with marsh marigolds, to a downhill segment via glacially modelled slabs. One the edge of beech woods facing the lower southern slope of Monte Orsaro ('bear mountain') is a path junction at 1600m (45min) in sight of the hut **Capanna del Braiola**; another original place name dating back to Lombard times, a reference to 'free pasture'.

Unless you have the extra time and energy to take on the rewarding 1830m ridge peak in addition to the day's load, then turn R (N) on n.727.

Not far downhill, fork L on n.727a, a gentle climb on a pleasant broad mule track with stone embankments. It gains the wooded ridge and proceeds on a level to the foot of Monte Fosco – drop R past an access path from Lagdei, sticking to the mule track (n.725a/723) over a soft carpet of pine needles. Back once more on the main ridge is one of a series of curious stone pillars bearing the crown denoting the erstwhile border of the Duchy of Parma at

1hr 50min – Bocchetta del Tavolo (1444m) where n.725 from Rifugio Lagdei joins up.

Due N n.00 leads through to a clearing thick with raspberries (ignore the fork for Monte Tavola). Scenic meadows coloured by meadow saffron and frequented by birds of prey are crossed, then it's back to shady squirrel-infested woodland in decided descent to a succession of grassy knolls. A graceful Romanesque-style chapel is passed, a deceptively recent construction that occupies the site of a historic hospice. From here a lane leads to nearby

40min – Passo di Cirone (1265m). Long known to smugglers, in the late 1800s the pass also saw the passage of skilled timber workers on their way to Corsica to fashion sleepers for the railway.

About 1km along to the R is renowned seafood restaurant and snack bar Faro Rosso. Should you need to leave the Trek here, take the quiet SP 18 road E for the 6km to the village of Bosco (see Stage 22 for practicalities).

Keep straight ahead, around the traffic barrier and onto a jeep track N through flowered fields with sweeping views R (E) over Val Parma and L (SW) towards the coast. A matter of minutes on, with the roof of the restaurant visible, leave the track for a path R. Waymarks soon reappear as you pass beneath a crumbling outcrop, stronghold of grey hooded crows. Stick to n.00 as it is joined by a track then follows a fence, bearing W.

Some 40min from Passo di Cirone, immediately after a makeshift livestock gate, leave the track for the faint path L uphill. A barbed-wire fence needs burrowing under, prior to the 10min climb up **Monte Beccara** or Buccaro (1379m) and another historic if weather-worn sandstone marker. Marvellous views which will hopefully take in the Alps across the mugginess of the Po plain, in addition to the raised motorway above Pontremoli. Moreover the mountains ahead are gentler and lower in altitude from here on, the dramatic ridge and peaks left behind. The mountains drop away SW towards La Spezia and the Tyrrhenian coast, while NE are the undulating hills of Parma ham-and-cheese country.

A slight dip then more panoramic crest NW to **Monte Fontanini** (1401m), then Passo della Cisa is clearly seen. A rutted track along the sinuous crest leads N through pasture in gradual descent to a conspicuous saddle at the foot of the elongated Groppo del Vescovo rock formation. (At the time of writing, the

Old marker near Monte Beccaro and view to Passo della Cisa

Pontremoli–Parma gas pipeline was being put through here, but the trenches will presumably be filled in and only faint traces left; in any case only a short stretch of path was affected.)

Proceed on n.00 and WNW in a quick climb to the rear of the rock ridge. A faint path crosses raspberry patches and pasture bright with orange lilies, abundant despite the abundance of cows, to

1hr 40min – Groppo del Vescovo (1243m), the 'bishop's mount'.

Following a fence, n.00 heads downhill to another jeep track and 1176m pass.

Note: At this point the Trek departs from the GEA as the paths have become overgrown, obliterated and/or fallen into disuse, thus unfeasible.

Take care not to go straight up the other side this time, but keep slightly L of the main crest (still n.00) cutting through trees back up to the top. Enjoying wide-ranging views it heads along the edge of a conifer plantation to power lines on Monte Valoria (1229m) and masses of gorgeous thistles. Here it is joined by the Via Francigena. Descending gently into mixed woodland of hazel and oak, a broad lane takes over further on and you coast easily into

1hr – Passo della Cisa (1041m), named for the Latin for 'cut' as the Romans put a road through. Snack bars, restaurants, souvenirs galore. If you're ready to call it a day at this point, 1.5km L (S) down the SS62, Locanda degli Aceri tel: 0187 436171 offers good-value accommodation; moreover the restaurant serves unusual local dishes such as flavoursome testaroli al pesto, pasta squares served with a fragrant sauce, a clear sign that you're on the doorstep of Liguria. In the opposite direction, 9km away, Berceto has ⓘ tel: 0525 64764 and Hotel Vittoria tel: 0525 64306, and regular daily bus

Passo della Cisa

services to Parma. The village can be reached by bus if you arrange beforehand for a pick-up at the pass – see *Pronto Bus* in Introduction.

Straight after the eateries, cross the road and take the steps R (W) past the grey stone church dedicated to Nostra Signora della Guardia, built in 1921 on what used to be a customs post. Keep L for the path along the crest into woodland. About 12min on, immediately after a clearing, keep your eyes peeled for faint red/white paint splashes and a path that leaves the main route (**Note**: It is not shown on most maps). It has no numbering but occasionally bears a pilgrim figure denoting the Via Francigena. With a fair few ups and downs, it heads essentially S. A landslip gully needs to be clambered across, nothing of consequence at the time of writing. The path drops gradually around the wooded hillside of Monte Zuchello, parallel to the road which remains out of sight. A marshy patch preceeds a track which is abandoned at a minor watercourse. Sweet-scented pine forest characterises the subsequent section, then you join the route of an older *condotta interrata*, 'underground pipeline'.

Emerging on the road the path soon reaches **Passo del Righetto** (973m), recognisable by a tight curve in the road. The path heads off R (SW) to plunge through drier wood that alternates with marshy patches thick with pungent wild mint. You clamber over a stony watercourse and soon turn L on an old overgrown lane enclosed by dry stone walls. Go R at the nearby surfaced road but a couple of minutes along take the path R around a playing field, for a final inconsequential climb. You emerge opposite the church at

1hr 30min – Montelungo (822m). Quiet village with attractive laid-back Hotel Appennino tel: 0187 436131; while a tad overpriced in terms of lodging, its al fresco restaurant is great value. It prides itself on its traditional Lunigiana specialities such as torta d'erbe (a flavoursome savoury flan of seasonal vegetables) and succulent grilled agnello (lamb). Basic rooms for rent can also be arranged through the nearby snack bar tel: 0187 436126.

The church above Passo della Cisa and view back over the route

The Trek ends at Montelungo and this comfortable old-style hotel

Year-round bus service (except Suns and hols) to the railhead Pontremoli which boasts a graceful medieval bridge and an important museum with prehistoric anthropomorphic stele statues, the oldest dating back to 3000BC; ⓘ tel: 0187 833287.

A wonderful follow-up is to head for La Spezia and spend time lazing on the famous spectacular Cinque Terre coast, or taking the dizzy pathways along the breathtaking terraces.

ROUTE SUMMARY

hrs
0 — Bocca Trabaria
1 — Passo delle Vacche
2
3
4 — Pian delle Capanne
5
6 — Passo di Viamaggio
7 — fork Eremo di Cerbaiolo
8 — Pieve S. Stefano
9
10
11 — Caprese Michelangelo
12 — Fragaiolo
13 — Eremo La Casella
14
15 — Chiusi La Verna
— La Verna sanctuary
16
17
18 — Poggio Tre Vescovi
19
20
21 — Passo dei Mandrioli
22 — Badia Prataglia

hrs
22 — Badia Prataglia
23
24 — Prato alla Penna
— Eremo di Camaldoli
25 — Camaldoli
26 — Eremo di Camaldoli
27
28 — Poggio Scali
29
30 — Passo della Calla
31 — La Burraia
— Monte Falco
32
33 — Giogo di Castagno
34
35 — Passo del Muraglione
36 — Colla della Maestà
37 — Giogo di Corella
38
39
40 — Poggio degli Allocchi
41 — Colla di Casaglia
42
43 — Passo Sambuca
44

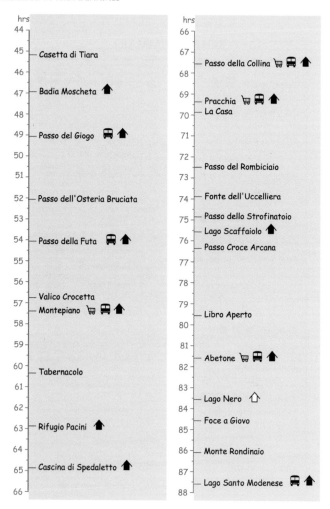

hrs

44 —
45 — Casetta di Tiara
46 —
47 — Badia Moscheta
48 —
49 — Passo del Giogo
50 —
51 —
52 — Passo dell'Osteria Bruciata
53 —
54 — Passo della Futa
55 —
56 —
57 — Valico Crocetta
— Montepiano
58 —
59 —
60 — Tabernacolo
61 —
62 —
63 — Rifugio Pacini
64 —
65 — Cascina di Spedaletto
66 —

hrs

66 —
67 — Passo della Collina
68 —
69 — Pracchia
70 — La Casa
71 —
72 — Passo del Rombiciaio
73 —
74 — Fonte dell'Uccelliera
75 — Passo dello Strofinatoio
— Lago Scaffaiolo
76 — Passo Croce Arcana
77 —
78 —
79 — Libro Aperto
80 —
81 —
— Abetone
82 —
83 —
— Lago Nero
84 — Foce a Giovo
85 —
86 — Monte Rondinaio
87 —
88 — Lago Santo Modenese

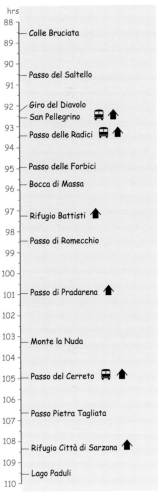

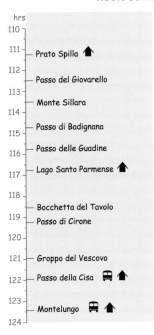

hrs
- 88 — Colle Bruciata
- 89
- 90
- 91 — Passo del Saltello
- 92 — Giro del Diavolo
- San Pellegrino
- 93 — Passo delle Radici
- 94
- 95 — Passo delle Forbici
- 96 — Bocca di Massa
- 97 — Rifugio Battisti
- 98
- 99 — Passo di Romecchio
- 100
- 101 — Passo di Pradarena
- 102
- 103 — Monte la Nuda
- 104
- 105 — Passo del Cerreto
- 106
- 107 — Passo Pietra Tagliata
- 108 — Rifugio Città di Sarzana
- 109
- 110 — Lago Paduli

hrs
- 110
- 111 — Prato Spilla
- 112 — Passo del Giovarello
- 113 — Monte Sillara
- 114 — Passo di Badignana
- 115
- 116 — Passo delle Guadine
- 117 — Lago Santo Parmense
- 118 — Bocchetta del Tavolo
- 119 — Passo di Cirone
- 120
- 121 — Groppo del Vescovo
- 122 — Passo della Cisa
- 123 — Montelungo
- 124

137

ITALIAN–ENGLISH GLOSSARY

abbazia	abbey
acqua non controllata	water not analysed for drinking
acqua (non) potabile	water (not) suitable for drinking
addestramento cani da caccia	training ground for hunting dogs
affittacamere	rooms to rent
agriturismo	farm with meals and/or accommodation
albergo	hotel
alimentari	grocery shop
alloggio	accommodation
alto	high, upper
aperto	open
area attrezzata	picnic area
autostazione	bus, coach station
autostrada	toll-paying motorway
badia	abbey
bandita di caccia	no hunting
basso	low, lower
bestiame al pascolo	livestock grazing
biglietto	ticket
biglietteria	ticket office
bocca	pass, literally 'mouth'
bosco	wood
caccia	hunting
camera, stanza	room
campeggio permesso/vietato	camping allowed/forbidden
capanna	hut
carta escursionistica	walking map
castello	castle
centro visita	visitors' centre
chiesa	church
chiudere il cancello	close the gate
chiuso	closed
colle, colla	pass
collina	hill
crinale	main ridge
croce	cross, crucifix
diga	dam
divieto di accesso/caccia	entry/hunting forbidden
enoteca	wine bar, shop
entrata	entry
eremo	monastic retreat, hermitage
fermata di autobus	bus stop
fiume	river

fonte, sorgente	spring, fountain
foresta demaniale	state forest
foresteria	accommodation at a monastery
frazione	hamlet
giogo	pass, literally 'yoke'
groppo	knoll
grotta	cave
lago	lake
maneggio	horse-riding
maestà	wayside shrine, tabernacle
metanodotto	gas pipeline
montagna, monte	mountain
mulattiera	mule track
museo	museum
ostello	hostel
osteria	tavern
palestra di roccia	rock-climbing practice wall
panificio	bakery
pericolo/pericoloso	danger/dangerous
pieve	village
poggio	hill, knoll
ponte	bridge
posto tappa	walker's accommodation
prato	meadow
proprietà privata	private property
ricovero invernale	refuge winter premises
rifugio	mountain refuge for walkers
santuario	sanctuary, hermitage
sbocco	pass
seggiovia	chair lift
segheria	sawmill
segnaletica	waymarking
sella	saddle
sentiero	path
sentiero attrezzato	aided path (with fixed cables)
sentiero natura	nature trail
stazione ferroviaria	railway station
strada	road
strada forestale	forestry track
strada sterrata	unsealed road
supermercato	supermarket
tabernacolo	tabernacle, shrine
torrente	stream
trattoria	restaurant
uscita	exit
uso cucina	kitchen facilities
valico	pass
viottolo	country lane
vipera	viper, adder

LISTING OF CICERONE GUIDES

NORTHERN ENGLAND
LONG-DISTANCE TRAILS
The Dales Way
The Reiver's Way
The Alternative Coast to Coast
The Coast to Coast Walk
The Pennine Way
Hadrian's Wall Path
The Teesdale Way

FOR COLLECTORS OF SUMMITS
The Relative Hills of Britain
Mts England & Wales Vol 2 –
England
Mts England & Wales Vol 1 – Wales

BRITISH CYCLE GUIDES
The Cumbria Cycle Way
Lands End to John O'Groats – Cycle
Guide
On the Ruffstuff: 84 Bike Rides in
North England
Rural Rides No.1 – West Surrey
Rural Rides No.2 – East Surrey
South Lakeland Cycle Rides
Border Country Cycle Routes
Lancashire Cycle Way

CANOE GUIDES
Canoeist's Guide to the North-East

LAKE DISTRICT AND
MORECAMBE BAY
Coniston Copper Mines
Scrambles in the Lake District
More Scrambles in the Lake District
Walks in Silverdale and
Arnside AONB
Short Walks in Lakeland 1 – South
Short Walks in Lakeland 2 – North
Short Walks in Lakeland 3 – West
The Tarns of Lakeland Vol 1 – West
The Tarns of Lakeland Vol 2 – East
The Cumbria Way &
Allerdale Ramble
Winter Climbs in the Lake District
Roads and Tracks of the Lake District
The Lake District Angler's Guide
Rain or Shine – Walking in the
Lake District
Rocky Rambler's Wild Walks
An Atlas of the English Lakes

NORTH-WEST ENGLAND
Walker's Guide to the
Lancaster Canal
Walking in Cheshire
Family Walks in the
Forest Of Bowland
Walks in Ribble Country
Historic Walks in Cheshire
Walking in Lancashire
Walks in Lancashire Witch Country
The Ribble Way

THE ISLE OF MAN
Walking on the Isle of Man
The Isle of Man Coastal Path

PENNINES AND
NORTH-EAST ENGLAND
Walks in the Yorkshire Dales – Vol 1
Walking in the South Pennines
Walking in the North Pennines
The Yorkshire Dales
Walks in the North York Moors –
Vol 1
Walks in the North York Moors –
Vol 2
Walking in the Wolds
Waterfall Walks – Teesdale and High
Pennines
Walking in County Durham
Yorkshire Dales Angler's Guide
Backpacker's Britain – Northern
England
Walks in Dales Country
Historic Walks in North Yorkshire
South Pennine Walks
Walking in Northumberland

DERBYSHIRE, PEAK DISTRICT,
EAST MIDLANDS
High Peak Walks
White Peak Walks Northern Dales
White Peak Walks Southern Dales
White Peak Way
The Viking Way
Star Family Walks Peak District &
South Yorkshire
Walking In Peakland
Historic Walks in Derbyshire

WALES AND WELSH BORDERS
Ascent of Snowdon
Welsh Winter Climbs
Hillwalking in Wales – Vol 1
Hillwalking in Wales – Vol 2
Scrambles in Snowdonia
Hillwalking in Snowdonia
The Ridges of Snowdonia
Hereford & the Wye Valley
Walking Offa's Dyke Path
The Brecon Beacons
Lleyn Peninsula Coastal Path
Anglesey Coast Walks
The Shropshire Way
Spirit Paths of Wales
Glyndwr's Way
The Pembrokeshire Coastal Path
Walking in Pembrokeshire
The Shropshire Hills – A Walker's
Guide
Backpacker's Britain Vol 2 – Wales

MIDLANDS
The Cotswold Way
West Midlands Rock
The Grand Union Canal Walk
Walking in Oxfordshire
Walking in Warwickshire
Walking in Worcestershire
Walking in Staffordshire
Heart of England Walks

SOUTHERN ENGLAND
The Wealdway & the Vanguard Way
Exmoor & the Quantocks
Walking in the Chilterns
Walks in Kent Book 2
Two Moors Way
Walking in Dorset
Walking in Cornwall
A Walker's Guide to the Isle of
Wight
Walking in Devon
Walking in Somerset
The Thames Path
Channel Island Walks
Walking in Buckinghamshire
The Isles of Scilly
Walking in Hampshire
Walking in Bedfordshire
The Lea Valley Walk
Walking in Berkshire
The Definitive Guide to
Walking in London
The Greater Ridgeway
Walking on Dartmoor
The South West Coast Path
Walking in Sussex
The North Downs Way
The South Downs Way

SCOTLAND
Scottish Glens 1 – Cairngorm Glens
Scottish Glens 2 – Atholl Glens
Scottish Glens 3 – Glens of Rannoch
Scottish Glens 4 – Glens of Trossach
Scottish Glens 5 – Glens of Argyll
Scottish Glens 6 – The Great Glen
Scottish Glens 7 – The Angus Glens
Scottish Glens 8 – Knoydart
to Morvern
Scottish Glens 9 – The Glens
of Ross-shire
Scrambles in Skye
The Island of Rhum
Torridon – A Walker's Guide
Ski Touring in Scotland
Walking the Galloway Hills
Walks from the West Highland
Railway
Border Pubs & Inns –
A Walkers' Guide
Walks in the Lammermuirs
Scrambles in Lochaber
Walking in the Hebrides
Central Highlands: 6 Long
Distance Walks
Walking in the Isle Of Arran
Walking in the Lowther Hills
North to the Cape
The Border Country –
A Walker's Guide
Winter Climbs – Cairngorms
The Speyside Way
Winter Climbs – Ben Nevis &
Glencoe
The Isle of Skye, A Walker's Guide